THE TAFT STORY

THE TAFT STORY

by

WILLIAM S. WHITE

Illustrated

HARPER & ROW, PUBLISHERS

New York

All photographs appearing in the book by Wide World, Inc.

To my mother, Mrs. John Van Dyke White
(Lucia Alberta Smith White)

ACKNOWLEDGMENTS

To Caroline Thomas Harnsberger and her book, *A Man of Courage*, I am indebted for an able genealogy of the Taft family and for an anecdote dealing with Robert A. Taft's early youth. My obligation in similar connections to Mrs. Darrah Wunder is great.

I owe much, likewise, to many public men (none of whom must on any account be held responsible for any conclusion in this book) and more specifically to Mr. Herbert Hoover, Governor Dewey of New York, Ambassador Henry Cabot Lodge and White House officials Jack Martin and James Hagerty.

To my wife, June, my debt is greatest of all.

CONTENTS

CONTENTS

IV

The Last, Best Taft

A section of illustrations appears following page 86.

I.

THE FUNDAMENTAL TAFT

☆ 1 ☆

CINCINNATI DYNASTY

In Cincinnati, a sedate, withdrawn and rather ingrown city behind the wall of the Ohio River, most of the best people mourn, in an offhand, well-bred way, a man they had known for forty years or so and had not in fact known at all. Senator Robert A. Taft came from Cincinnati in the most exact meaning of that phrase. He was from it, but not of it, and though it was reasonably correct to call him "Mr. Republican" and not too far out to call him "Mr. Congress" no one could sensibly have called him "Mr. Cincinnati," or "Mr. Ohio" either, for that matter.

The most casual inquiry among Mr. Taft's peers in Cincinnati—the brokers, bankers, corporation lawyers and the like who used to see him stalk unseeingly into and out of the Queen City Club—makes it abundantly clear that this was not really his home. Their views of him are tight, tidy, enormously assured—and profoundly oversimplified and wrong.

They had, and have, a series of images as neat and as uninforming as a panel of photographs of the kind that one sometimes sees in old family albums—the smiling infant, the boy just setting off for the first time to school, the young man in blazer at college and, finally, the mature man standing at the center of his own family.

They think of him—the "right people" of Cincinnati, and these were the only ones who knew him even in an uncomprehending way—as the fit and perfect embodiment of the bloodless minor virtues of the business community of Cincinnati and by their projection of the business community of America. They recall proudly that when he was up there on the sixth floor of the Dixie Terminal Building as partner in the law firm of Taft, Stettinius and Hollister he almost never made a mistake in handling the stocks and bonds of his clients.

They remember with great distinctness that he always knew better than to mix with the reformers of Cincinnati, those who to this day are called "Charterites," partly because the Charter altered Cincinnati's form of government to take in a city manager but mostly because in Cincinnati if one is not an "Organization" Republican one is a "Charterite." It is not illegal to be a Democrat in Cincinnati but it is at best faintly disreputable. To this extent, therefore, the Charter movement may be said to supply an essential rationale. This is how in local affairs one objects to the patina of early McKinleyism that still covers the orthodox Republicans in Cincinnati without having to go so immeasurably far as to take the Democratic vows.

The fact is that from the beginning of his political life Taft took his stand firmly with the orthodox, not necessarily in total hostility to the dreams of the reformers and new thinkers of his various eras but because he simply could not, emotionally or intellectually, countenance the slightest deviation within any organization.

All this was conditioned, of course, by the memories held by Robert A. Taft of what deviationism had done to another Taft, his father, William Howard, because of a Roosevelt, Theodore. The year 1912 lived to the end in the recollections of the son, for it was in 1912 that William Howard Taft was defeated for re-election to the Presidency by Woodrow Wilson with the decisive aid of Theodore Roosevelt's then third party, the bolting Bull Moose.

This episode did not cause Robert Taft to hate the Bull Moose—probably because as Brother Charles P. Taft observes, "We Tafts are not much on hating." But it had on Robert Taft something of the effect that a mutiny within a company of troops would have on the son of an Army officer who himself was then in training at West Point to become an officer, too. It made Robert Taft deeply fear any disorder in the ranks and to regard the promotion of disorder as approaching a crime, if an unconscious one.

Taft the elder, that vast, jovial, convivial man, was in many respects a world away from the spare, shy, introspective Robert, but not a whit apart in the cardinal creed: Republicans must always stay Republicans.

Because all this was so Robert Taft never had great political trust in his brother, Charles. Indeed when "Charlie" was running for Governor of Ohio in 1952 "Senator Bob" never helpfully intervened until Charlie had won the Republican nomination on his own, and gave only rather formalized aid even in the general election campaign.

Bob Taft understood, and Charles Taft understands: The divergence in Cincinnati, where in many quarters Charles is definitely the Wrong Taft, was similar in a way to the convulsions within dynasties that Europe sometimes knew in the last eras of the personal kings, where it was sometimes historically impossible for Monarch A to come to the succor of cousin or brother as Monarch B.

This was all the more the case in the instance of the Taft dynasty; or, to change the expression, of the Taft family, that lives a kind of Galsworthian Forsyte Saga in Cincinnati. Robert Taft not only was unhappily and deeply convinced of the unwisdom of some of Charles' politics and habits—which included intimate associations with such Eastern internationalist Republicans as the late Henry L. Stimson and actual friendship with Dean Acheson—but Charles Taft never hesitated to break with "the Organization."

Robert Taft loved his brother Charles, for he was after all and beyond question a Taft, but here were situations that went before personal relationships, however deep and valued. The late King George VI of Britain may be fairly assumed not to have approved certain actions of his brother Edward VIII, if only because these actions were clearly not in accord with the life and traditions of their father, old George V.

In the same spirit, Bob Taft approached with sorrow but with determined disapproval many of the political activities of brother Charlie. He was aseptically firm. For example, on a television panel show while the 1952 primary campaign in Ohio was coming to crisis, Glenn Thompson of the Cincinnati *Enquirer* put to Senator Taft the soft-voiced but embarrassingly pertinent question:

"Senator, are you going to support your brother Charlie?"

Facing the eyes of God knows how many viewers in how many Sunday-afternoon living rooms, Senator Taft replied, with the tart impatience under which he always hid emotion and regret, to this effect:

"Mr. Thompson, I will not interfere in Republican primaries." The answer came from a man who was himself involved in a big affair, what turned out to be his last unsuccessful run for the Presidential nomination, and so it could have been motivated by personal political considerations alone. I myself do not think so, though; this was simply the inevitable response of Taft the Organization man.

At all events, it was not understood—this time either inside or outside of Cincinnati—for, again, it was a reply based not so much in disapproval of Charles Taft's liberal ideas as in disapproval of Charles Taft's clear intention to buck the Republican powers in Cincinnati and Ohio. With any sort of blessing from them, Charlie could have had anything Bob had.

These Republican powers in Cincinnati exist in the past just as does the city itself, despite its great growth and the influx of outsiders since the Second World War. Robert Taft came early among the powers, bringing the not typical Cincinnati background of a young man who had lived with stolid studiousness in the White House and had won honors at Yale and then at Harvard Law.

He entered politics in Cincinnati in 1920 in what by

Taftians is called "the hard way," though it was hardly insupportably difficult for the son of William Howard Taft, with all that this meant in Cincinnati. That is, he became a Republican precinct captain and did his stint at bell-ringing, though, again, it is not likely that many Republican doors— in a city of Republican doors—left these summonses unanswered.

In 1921, as was more or less foreordained, he took the next, correct step in this early political minuet. He was elected to the Ohio legislature, became successively Republican floor leader and Speaker of the House. In 1930 he was elected to the Ohio State Senate. In 1932 an insistent advocacy of Herbert Hoover for the Presidency brought Taft defeat for re-election to the State Senate and put him forever in a kind of glad political thrall to Mr. Hoover, with whose relief administration he had served in Europe in 1917–1919.

This association became one of the most meaningful in Taft's long career; he never afterward gave up on Mr. Hoover, and Mr. Hoover reciprocated fully. In the last, hot hours at the Chicago Republican national convention in July of 1952 the Taft headquarters, facing imminent and heavy defeat from the Eisenhower partisans, rather movingly brought forth a strong Taft-for-President endorsement from the aged ex-President Hoover.

Taft's long discipleship, in many ways, of Mr. Hoover had perhaps come because Mr. Hoover was somewhat, but not too much, like the Cincinnati Organization. It was characteristic of the Senator, who had a view of Mr. Hoover as perhaps the most eminently suitable of all Republicans, that he should not recognize at this moment that Hoover's was a voice from the long past and, rightly or wrongly, not very relevant at Chicago in 1952.

The incident was a fairly good clue to Taft's own bleak romance with tradition. As he stood early and to the end with Mr. Hoover he stood early and to the end in Ohio with heavy-handed politicians who, in simple fact, enormously handicapped him every time he went out for the Presidential nomination. He stood with Mr. Hoover, however, in the belief that Hoover represented the best. He stood with many of his Ohio managers or submanagers in full private awareness of their shortcomings, including their almost perfect unawareness of Republican sentiment outside the Middle West, only out of a kind of excessive, if cool, loyalty to the Organization, its personnel, and even its prejudices.

It is not that all these prejudices were shared by him—many, including orthodox Ohio Republicanism's far more sour view of the round world—were never his own. It was simply that he forgave or overlooked the actions and attitudes of men about him in a strangely naïve belief that if ignored these actions and attitudes would somehow go away out of sight. Personal fondness, a personal commitment of friendship by Taft, were involved in some of these cases; but to my knowledge certainly not in all.

Taft had a certain feeling of *noblesse oblige* to all who served him, however poorly, so long as they had been a long time at it, and a private generosity of which few knew and which he honestly tried to keep dourly hidden. When he left his desk at Taft, Stettinius and Hollister and turned it over

to "Young Bob" Taft, the son found it filled with I O U's that
had never been collected and never would be, by the Senator's strict injunction. The right people in Cincinnati thought,
as they think now, that the Senator had a satisfactorily
mercantile view toward life and his own law practice. This
was not the case. He guarded the portfolios of others with
an almost savage meticulousness; but this was not because
they *were* portfolios but because they belonged to others.

Taft's own attitude toward his own money—which actually
was not too considerable, since his total estate would hardly
run above $500,000—was simply this: It was natural, indeed
inevitable, that he should have adequate money, but it was
not too important. Other men, some of them other Tafts, in
a financial way always underwrote his political ambitions as
they had for his father before him. He thought this only
right and proper.

The fact is, too, he put a great deal less emphasis on
money as part of a political campaign than more liberal
politicians have done. Once, as he approached a heavy test
in standing for re-election to the Senate in 1950, a friend
asked him whether the national Republican organization
would help him in a money way. "*Money,*" he said incredulously. "What do you think I need with that? There's always plenty of that for me." He even made an occasional,
irreverent joke about what the political trade calls "fat cats."
I found that a recollection of this did not amuse some of
Taft's old associates in Cincinnati; they were pained and
unbelieving when this anecdote was told of him.

He drove a small and inexpensive car—usually a Plymouth

or another in that general price range, and both in Washington and in Cincinnati he drove for himself, often erratically, for he never could put his mind on such matters. Mack Gray, the Senator's colored houseman, gave a good description of Taft's private manner.

"Never saw a man like Senator," said Mack. "You take something like breakfast. He come down in the morning. He sit down at the table and he takes out his little book and writes in it—every morning he writes and writes in it. I say, 'Good morning, Senator.' No answer. I go out of the room and bring in the coffee. I go out again and bring in the cereal. He still writing in that book. Finally, he looks up and says, 'Why, good morning, Mack,' like he is surprised to see me. He hadn't heard me at all.

"But then, say he is coming into Washington. I meet him at the train. He has his grip, I go to take it. 'No, no, Mack, I can carry it,' he says. 'I'll drive, too.' He drives and he scares me a little. You know: Whush. Whoof. Fast; and he hasn't got his mind on it. And when we get home to Georgetown he carries his own bag up three flights of steps. He didn't like anybody to do anything he could do hisself. Nobody knew that man too much; but I did. When he was getting ready to die with that cancer he laugh and joke all the time around the house so as not to worry Mrs. Taft or Mrs. Wunder [Darrah Wunder, perhaps the closest friend of the Taft family]. God, how could that man *laugh* at a time like that?"

It was not, of course, precisely this face, or even approximately this face, that Taft turned to his Queen City Club kind of associates in Cincinnati and/or the Organization people. Though he was often with them, and had been often with some of them for nearly a lifetime, he had no intimacy with them nor they with him. Sometimes he would pass one or another of them on the street without speaking or breaking his stride.

The other man was not offended but rather pleased with this; it comported exactly with his idea of the proper public man, standing aside and away and preoccupied with high thoughts. Taft once went to Florida to a pre-Presidential convention gathering arranged by a Cincinnati Organization man to impress a great many powerful Republicans who were down there for the Season. The Senator spoke his piece and walked quickly out a side door, shaking never a hand of the eight hundred that were there to be shaken.

This, of course, was in no sense good politics; but the Taft people thought it quite wonderful. It is still spoken of in Cincinnati as illustrating the profound "solidity" of Taft's character. What it was, of course, was something very different. It illustrated the great shyness with which Taft had lived all his life and toward which he had begun only in his last years to make some sort of softening accommodation.

But this was the way he went in all his political years in Cincinnati—aloof, a political necessity to the Organization, which thought of him in many ways as he was not. One of his earliest associates says that Taft never had taken a step in his life since his twentieth year that was not already interrelated in his mind with steps that would be taken, in due course, many years hence. This, it seems to me, is a right judgment, but only to a degree.

Taft's long objection to "planning," a word that along with the word "Democrat" he always made to sound slightly theatrical and dubious, was sometimes not inconsistent with his own conduct. Though he did not do so in Cincinnati on any known or important occasion, there were many occasions in Washington when he moved in every way that was *not* according to plan.

And other old Taft associates in Cincinnati and elsewhere thought of him, and still do, as the one Republican who, in the White House, would infallibly cut all expenditures and end many, especially for such things as foreign aid, with some dramatic and implacable decision. They might have found themselves frustrated and unbelieving if ever he had become President. For apart from the fact that his sense of property was not nearly so acute as theirs his mind was infinitely more hospitable to ideas, in the sense of being willing at least to listen to them—ideas some of which were surpassingly strange to Cincinnati and never forced directly by him upon the community that typified so little of him.

Upper-crust Cincinnati is filled, in a relative sense, with Tafts, and all of Cincinnati is filled with Taft memorials or memories of one kind or another—Taft Museum, Taft roads, and so on. But the Taft family is not, in a good many ways, filled with or pervaded by Cincinnati. To some extent it exists on a plane that while horizontal to the city rises above and apart from it. The man who is probably the most likely long-term investment to carry on the Taft political dynasty, "Young Bob," has quietly taken his place in the old Taft law firm and serves there with due decorum toward his elders.

But Young Bob, like all the other Tafts, understands what the Taft peers do not understand about the Senator. If and when Young Bob takes up where his father did the Organization is almost certain to accept him but no more likely to dominate him than it did his father.

Lloyd Taft, another son, has, with equal propriety, put his career into the Cincinnati *Times-Star,* in which Senator Taft owned five per cent of the stock. The *Times-Star,* which is thought to be worth about ten million dollars, is headed by Mr. Hulbert Taft. Hulbert Taft was reasonably in touch with Senator Taft, but the two branches of the family are not necessarily one fold, except in confronting outsiders. The meetings of the *Times-Star* board are formidable gatherings, when the Taft and allied clans come together. It is an amusing irony that the fortune of the Tafts rests in part upon an activity and a profession about which Senator Taft had many misgivings, that is, the publication of the news.

Martha Taft, the Senator's widow, lives in gallantly suppressed grief in the Senator's rambling, softly beautiful home on Indian Hill, thirteen miles by road from Cincinnati and a much greater distance in other senses. The Senator is buried nearby in the Indian Hill Episcopal churchyard, in a rolling, leafy place near the Ohio River almost perfectly isolated from noise or movement.

Indian Hill, though suburban in the sense of location, is no Westchester County appendage to the metropolis. It was the setting not of an Ohio politician or a famous "Cincinnatian" but of a man of the nation, who once told me, square in the presence of a subordinate Ohio politician who was pressing the Taft ear with local problems: "Excuse me a minute; we have all got to deal [the word "deal" was clearly used to translate as "waste our time"] with this sort of thing."

It could fairly be said of Taft that to "this sort of thing" he owed no special debt. He was the son of a privilege that encompassed far more than Cincinnati or all Ohio, just as was Franklin Roosevelt of Hyde Park in his way, and he was well aware of this. Cincinnati, in this sense, was the place from which Taft took the train to Washington. If he was ever sentimental about that place, I never saw a sign of it, for he had the opinion that nothing much was ever settled in all the Cincinnatis but only at the seat of the Federal power.

At this seat contended the mighty forces that with startling occasional private demonstrations of an acid objectivity he loved alike to watch in motion and to participate in.

☆ 2 ☆

TAFT AND INTEGRITY

W hen Robert A. Taft was about nineteen years old his father, William Howard Taft, then President, was returning to Washington from a Western trip. Robert, then at Yale, telegraphed the White House with characteristic deliberation of purpose that he would be on hand to greet the President. Gravely he made his way to Washington but at the station he omitted to say who he was. When the train came in, the stationmaster waved off young Bob, saying: "You'll have to get back, young fellow. This space is reserved for officials who are meeting the President."

Bob slipped off into the crowd and had to be hunted out by the Presidential party. He was, so the family anecdote runs, quite without resentment.

This was the Robert Taft who, soon after arriving in Washington in 1939 as a United States Senator from Ohio, began calmly and rather absently to thrust his way forward, in a place where newcomers are put under the iciest pressure to mind their elders and to earn their seniority always in meekness and, so far as may be, in silence.

The Taft who had obediently gone back into the crowd at the station in 1908 was not overly humble; the incident simply had no importance to him. He had always a great dis-

like of conversation about trifles, an exercise he could barely
tolerate with associates and simply could not stomach at all
with strangers. He knew, of course, that in due time he
would join his father—and it is extremely unlikely that he
himself ever independently recalled the episode a month or
so after.

But the Taft who pushed his way without apology—and
with what would have been unseemly haste in another—to
the top of that most patriarchal body, the Senate, was the
same Taft. This time, it was simply that he was seen in
exigent and important circumstances.

The nature of the Senate, which mysteriously accepts and
mysteriously rejects the newly arriving, helped him to the
extent that not even his earliest years there are remembered
by old colleagues as indicating any Taft bumptiousness. But
it was primarily a long and complicated gathering of circumstances, in this country and in the world at large, that put
Robert A. Taft so soon at the top of the Senate hierarchy.

Highly complex forces were rising abroad. There was
Hitler in Germany and there was Mussolini in Italy. Even as
to the Pacific some of the more acute public men in this
country were beginning to revise an old and favored notion
that Japan was a faintly comic-opera land where everybody
worshiped a curious little Emperor.

The Republican party in the United States had fallen upon
days that were of unexampled leanness; its diet was extremely thin. Franklin D. Roosevelt and the New Deal were
succeeding, from the orthodox Republican view, in actions
of unspeakable enormity in domestic affairs. One alphabet

agency—and how they were denounced!—was following another, and nobody knew where it would all end. Free enterprise was dying, so it was declared with endless forebodings among the Republicans, and the capitalist system itself was eroding away under the attrition of what Taft was later to begin calling socialism.

But perhaps worse still, Mr. Roosevelt and the men around him were, in the orthodox Republican notion, beginning a strange and desperately dangerous course in international affairs. Plainly, they were beginning to take sides, not only emotionally but in practical ways, with Britain. The threat of "the entangling alliance"—and everyone knew George Washington had warned against that—filled the air.

Moreover, the Republican party within itself was beginning to show alarming deviations and here and there outright hospitality to some of the New Deal designs. Few remember now, perhaps, that even so stanch a Midwest Republican figure as Senator Arthur H. Vandenberg of Michigan (this of course was long before his conversion to the interventionist side in world affairs) was being shaken now and then under the storms of Democratic innovations in the domestic field.

The 1936 Republican resistance to Roosevelt had been a dreary failure; Alf Landon of Kansas as the party's Presidential nominee had won precisely two states, the unshakable and storied Maine and Vermont.

In all this melancholy scene the hard-core Republicans of the United States began to turn inquiringly toward Senator Taft. It did not matter to them, nor were they by any means generally conscious, that Taft might not in every way and at every turn represent their fundamental policy of no change. They had seen the collapse of the build-up of Governor Landon, who had the heavy liability of living in a small and distant state and the heavier one of lacking prominence in the party. They knew that great forces were at work, and from these they sought safety.

Who, in these circumstances, could overlook Taft of Ohio? There was the famous name—a name redolent of the old, safe days of the Republican party and a name never touched in the remotest way with the aura of scandal that had arisen in the Harding Administration. And even though William Howard Taft *had* been defeated in 1912, the orthodox regarded this—as indeed did Robert Taft himself—as hardly a conscious decision by the United States. It was an irregularity; an aberration.

Thus Taft himself had not been thirty days in the Senate before, as the saying goes at political conventions, destiny had marked him. And in this case, the amiable cliché was also a statement of a fact. Taft, as he had become earlier to the Organization in Cincinnati, was becoming now a historical necessity to the Republican Organization of the United States. And that he was to the end.

The orthodox Republicans of the United States, then as now, *are* the Republicans, when one takes a slightly Taftian view of it, no matter how many times their choice may be rejected at national conventions. When all is lost, they hold the party together; without them the party would have rusted from disuse in the long Roosevelt era. When all is in a way won, as is currently the case in the nonorthodox Republican Administration of General Eisenhower, they work powerfully, endlessly, with great devotion and with considerable success to preserve at all costs the essential Republican creed. The ministry may change; at bottom the creed must remain.

They are found in every city and nearly every town—even in the more or less still one-party Democratic South—and though they go under millions of names their face is one. The orthodox Republican—that is, the Taft Republican— believes in stability, in order, in solvency as one of the highest of ends, in moving very slowly and changing almost never. He believes very much in tradition. He is not necessarily anti-intellectual (the fact is that Taft was an intellectual) but he much prefers that academic things, whether academic degrees or academic attitudes, not be talked about or used more than is absolutely necessary. The circumstance that Taft was both a Yale and a Harvard man, and moreover at Harvard had been editor of the *Law Review,* was never an asset to him except as to a very few and faintly deviationist members of the Republican orthodoxy, to whom these things were a comfort now and then.

Taft himself never stressed the academic side of his life and certainly not the Ivy League grand tour that had been in his background. In the Senate most of his closest professional associates were men who were anything but academic and were indeed disparate from him in a dozen ways but at one with him in the supreme thing. That is, they were all traditional Republicans who, like Taft himself, roamed only infrequently and briefly and always came home to the Old Guard.

When he arrived in the Senate in 1939, in a hard derby hat and wearing rimless glasses, he came with one moderately unusual credential apart from the inherent ones. In spite of his defeat for re-election to the Ohio State Senate in the Hoover debacle of 1932, the Ohio Organization had loyally put him up as a favorite son for the 1936 Presidential nomination that went at length to the unfortunate Governor Landon.

To be designated a favorite son means in politics almost precisely what it implies—that is, "Here is a man of whom we are proud." The Ohio Organization *was* proud of Taft, 1932 or no 1932. It paid him the honor by way of announcing that more would be heard of him and that, notwithstanding the recent reverses, he was still the best that Ohio had.

Though the prospect before Taft was far from bright for the Republicans, he was at once given seats on three of the most powerful committees of the Senate—Appropriations, Banking and Currency, and Labor. This came about partly because there were, relative to the present position, a great many more Republican committee places to be had. In a Senate of ninety-six members there were only twenty-three Republicans, among them indestructibles like William E. Borah of Idaho, and Hiram Johnson of California.

But Taft's recognition was primarily because he was a Taft and there was a curious fitness in the nature of the posts he got from the party satraps: Banking, Appropriations,

Labor. His great interest, then as always, really was in fiscal affairs and he put into his committee work the almost incredible concentration of cold energy that typified all his life, from the time he first went to Uncle Horace Taft's school in Watertown, Connecticut, in preparation for Yale.

It was here, amidst the Federal balance sheets and ledgers, the budgets and the bills, that Taft began to be in a small, concrete way as nearly indispensable to his party in fact as he became emotionally on the larger and grander scale. Though many people disagreed with his conclusions, few responsible men ever disputed the soundness of Taft's technique with figures.

At this time, back in his first Congress, the Seventy-sixth, he was no labor expert. The Republicans did not have much to do, in these years of the rampant Roosevelt, with labor legislation, except to view with great alarm. Taft had not, of course, become a fiscal expert overnight. From the beginning of his Senate service he was sitting in a body of men not one in ten of whom had even approximately the eye for finance that he had developed in Cincinnati. The Taft law office there was, and is, a reasonably close counterpart to a firm of British solicitors where property management is a far more common and useful function than appearances before the bench.

Through his industry, his great ability, his connections, his point of view and his rising utility, Taft got along well enough with the old formidables of the Senate. This was true of such as Borah and Hiram Johnson. He had, from the start, just the right sort of presence for his new job—gravity, solid-

ity, and an instinctive and perhaps in part inherited understanding of the habits and prejudices of this body where
he was to reach his highest distinction. And his great industry did no harm to him.

In the Senate—and this most of all was *his* place—Taft
pressed on fast through the Seventy-sixth Congress. By the
time it had ended the lasting stamp was upon him; he was
in 1940 what he had not been in 1936, a serious candidate
for the Republican Presidential nomination. At the 1940 convention in Philadelphia, the overwhelming choice of the
"safe" Republicans, he got caught by what really seemed,
through all his mature life, to have been a kind of negation
by fate.

His chosen opponent was Governor Thomas E. Dewey of
New York, but suddenly there appeared what was in Taft's
view another of the untidy improbabilities that pursued him
so long and so well. Though this was not for him the convention of supreme crisis—this crisis was to come in 1948 and
to repeat itself with finality in 1952—Philadelphia back in
1940 confronted Senator Taft with the kind of party disorder
that was intrinsically as well as expediently abhorrent to
him. As though Dewey had not been bad enough, here came
an outsider called Wendell Willkie—and flung forward, too,
by Easterners as Taft saw it, to balk him in the hour of possible triumph. There was a pointing finger in this incident,
a remarkable foreshadowing of what was to come in very
similar circumstances, and through planning from very similar sources, in 1952, the year that it was Eisenhower and not
Taft.

After Mr. Willkie's nomination and subsequent defeat by Franklin Roosevelt, Taft pulled himself together without great difficulty—he had a great, quiet appeal, as a man, in defeat—and went back to where he was at home, the Senate. Because of a commitment to a political associate, Senator John W. Bricker of Ohio, and faithful to the larger designs of the Organization in Ohio, Taft stayed in the shadows in 1944 and "let John try it."

"John" tried it, that is, for the Presidential nomination, and wound up as the Vice Presidential nominee on a ticket headed by that old Taft antagonist, Governor Dewey. No conceivable circumstance, by the way, could have persuaded Taft to take second place to Dewey.

Taft himself, who was oddly temperamental at times and by no means the cold rock of unvarying purpose that he was widely thought to have been, was up for re-election to the Senate from Ohio in that year, 1944. He did not greatly stir himself locally in Ohio and possibly because of this and his placarded hostility to Roosevelt and to Roosevelt's international policies he was saved only by tradition. He got back into office by 17,000 votes.

Still, he was back, and in the Senate memories of margins of victory are short and the recognition of the fact of victory is long. For the first time, Taft began really and openly to bestride that old chamber. In the first place, he represented then, as he did to the end of his life (and accurately led or reflected), far more private thought there than might be supposed. He was the beau ideal, if privately acknowledged in most cases, of nearly every Republican there—and many and many a Democrat.

In the campaign, so far as Mr. Roosevelt was involved, Taft had fought a fight of an almost savage candor. Where other Senators, particularly in the Democratic South, anathematized Roosevelt only in their hearts, he anathematized Roosevelt on the stump. By the very facts of the case, the continuing success of Roosevelt, the developing Democratic wartime policy that dealt gently with Stalin in order to dispose of Hitler, the orthodox Republicans began more and more to turn to Taft.

There grew about him a legend that was far more factual than not. Here began to arise the belief that later became a slogan, the belief that for the name Taft there was a synonym in the great English noun Integrity. And though there were points later at which this equation might have seemed a bit shaky, the slogan "Mr. Integrity" was fundamentally a truly applied one.

This is not to say that only Taft among the leading politicians had integrity; it is not to say that even the orthodox Republicans really believed that this was so. They knew that other Republicans had integrity, and a good deal of it. But they were frightened, and increasingly so as the years went on, that others with integrity seemed also to be moving away, leading ever larger bodies of followers, toward the most incredible accommodation of all. This, as they saw it, was an accommodation with the New Deal itself, at home *and* abroad.

But Taft's brand of integrity involved not simply a faith-fulness to orthodox Republican institutions and policies. Apart from this he had, as a public man, an attitude of integrity in the purely objective sense. Or, as Mr. Herbert Hoover once told this writer, Taft always acted, or intended to act, in this way: "First you must find the *facts*; then you must consider these in relation to the national experience." And in the personal sense Taft was, most of the time, a man almost aggressively unwilling to make even small com-promises with honesty. Once, a valued political lieutenant, Tom Coleman of Wisconsin, proudly carrying a warm tele-gram signed "Taft," cleared his throat and thanked the Senator for it. "Oh, that," said Taft. "Never saw that wire myself, you know. Martin [Jack Martin, his administrative assistant] sends those things out by the dozen."

While the intention is to deal later with the long struggle between Taft and Dewey, and all that they represented within the Republican party, it is worth stressing here the special orthodox Republican nightmare, a nightmare fear of a kind of illicit philosophic merger of Republicanism and the New and Fair Deals. This was and is at the heart of the profound antagonism of the Taftites for the Dewey people. More important for present purposes, it was from this night-mare that grew the compulsive, unalterable orthodox Re-publican belief that Taft not only had integrity but the special kind of integrity that would if necessary be prepared to destroy the whole Republican party before making any accommodation at all.

In this, the Taft Republicans nationally were as wrong in

their way, and with far graver implications of error, as were the unseeing Taft associates in Cincinnati who imagined that his bond folders were very high in his concern. For Taft as a conservative was in this respect a genuine conservator. Personally dogmatic he was, and most of the time at that. But it was never in him to put the torch to anything of value, however in his view that thing might have been perverted. Nevertheless, there was this strange sequence of events: The more the country's thinking seemed to be settling toward moderate liberalism and internationalism—and especially away from the isolationism that Taft was supposed to embody but usually did not—the more were gathered about him people who knew him less and less.

The mistake they made was cumulative and grew as he lived on. They thought that because there was one fixed constant in him—his institutional concern for the Republican party—his ideas and notions were fixed.

And even the reputation for integrity, though valid and though earned, should not be taken as too great an implied reproach to other politicians who never got that reputation, or at least not in capital letters. For Taft, as he himself casually recognized, was born to integrity as he was born to personal security. He never had to struggle for either.

3

THE BACKGROUND OF SHELTER

Without the slightest question Robert A. Taft was touched with the purple; in this case, the Taft family being what it was, the color was perhaps more a subdued mauve. He was born on September 8, 1889, in Cincinnati, in a house on East McMillan Street overlooking the Ohio River, the scion of a vast Taft clan that already had been eight generations in this country and had sprung from a land, Britain, whose motivations Senator Taft was to suspect off and on to the finish of his career.

The divisions and subdivisions of the family, which was founded in this country by another Robert Taft, whose first American home was in Braintree, Massachusetts, are quite bewildering to follow. The Tafts have always multiplied at a great rate—the original Robert Taft's five sons brought forth forty-five children—and a genealogical examination indicates that five children to a marriage would be about average.

Senator Taft and Martha Taft had four sons—William Howard Taft III, Robert, Jr., Lloyd and Horace. (William Howard III was chosen in 1953 by President Eisenhower to be Ambassador to Ireland, and both the choice of occupation and the place in which to practice it caused the Senator to raise a quizzical brow. He made it plain that *he* had nothing to do with this job; to friends who inquired about the appointment the Senator replied with an embarrassed smile: "Bill is on his own in this; absolutely on his own." Horace is a physicist and has been employed at the atomic weapon developments at Los Alamos.)

Robert A. Taft was an extraordinary boy, an oddly serious-looking little chap in his earliest photographs, who at the age of six began to make records of the distances traveled by the fire engines as they left and returned to the fire house across the street in Cincinnati. The firemen, no doubt awed at this enterprise, co-operated by giving him the data; he in turn prepared and presented to them at the end of twelve months his estimate of their activities for that period.

This little episode, apart from its singularity as indicating the concerns of a boy of six, is not without other interest. Always, or so it seemed, Taft preferred data to even the most fascinating of speculation and, in a way, even preferred facts to people in the mass. The debates he really relished in the Senate had to do with facts, the duller the better it sometimes appeared. Toward the end of his life I recall his visible happiness when briefly he could turn to his interest in such measurable matters as taxes and the detailed provisions of the Taft-Hartley labor act and put aside for a time the exasperating intangibles of his role as the Senate Republican leader.

His sense of basic aloneness, both from people and from their emotional as distinguished from their purely intellectual concerns, was illustrated when he was a student in college. George Fuller, a retired State Department career officer who was a member of Taft's Yale Class of 1910 and remained a lifelong friend, recalls that the development by this class of the "Whiffenpoof Song" left Robert A. Taft, the scholar, singularly unmoved.

If from time to time Taft was "down at Morey's," the famous tavern of the song, it was to have a few quiet glasses of beer in very nearly solitary state. He seems, as an undergraduate, to have found the song painfully sentimental; he lifted no glass to it at Morey's.

The future Senator's pursuits at Yale were almost exclusively mental, and mental in the bleakest sense. He *did* go out for the rowing crew, never making the varsity, but this though it involved a high degree of teamwork and stimulated a certain comradeship was not a particularly large-scale or mass activity. His fame lay then, as it did later, in his acts of cerebration. "Bob thought," as Fuller puts it, with an affectionate smile, "on a different level or plane from the rest of us. In those days, he always had the answers, and sometimes before one could put the questions."

The Taft critical powers were then, as always, quite active. "Once," says Fuller, "I decided to learn the violin and began to practice a lot in my room. Taft lived just above me. One night, as I was practicing, an alarm clock, ringing, was lowered on a string from Taft's room above to the level of my window. I decided to give up the violin."

To return to his beginnings. Robert Alphonso Taft's grandfather—who was, of course, the father of President William Howard Taft—was Alphonso Taft. Alphonso Taft founded the family in Cincinnati in 1838—after duly finishing with honors at Yale—in mild disenchantment with life in Ellington, Connecticut. Alphonso did not, however, proceed West with the gay and feckless venturesomeness associated with that period, or without money in his pocket.

He made it quite clear, according to the family records, that he was going West in some skepticism and proposed to live there only if this could be done in caution and in comfort. As he moved westward through New York and Pennsylvania, he wrote his father, Peter Rawson Taft, of his view of the city of New York:

"I dislike the character of the New York Bar exceedingly. The notorious selfishness and dishonesty of the great mass of men you find in New York is to my mind a serious obstacle to settling there."

Alphonso Taft accordingly moved on West. He stayed for a while in Zanesville, Ohio, passing the Ohio Bar examination there, and then wound up, quite solidly and for good, in Cincinnati. In 1841 he married Fannie Phelps of Vermont and the two of their five children who reached maturity were Charles Phelps Taft and Peter Rawson Taft II. Charles Phelps Taft inherited $50,000 from grandfather Phelps back East; moreover, Charles married the exceedingly wealthy Annie Sinton of Cincinnati.

Alphonso Taft had a good career at the law and was something of a diplomat. He served President Chester A. Arthur as Minister to Austria-Hungary and was American Minister to Russia. Nevertheless, he left an estate of a house and exactly $482.80. Alphonso Taft's second wife was Louisa (he

called her "Louise") Dutton of New Haven, and William
Howard Taft was the son of this marriage.

The William Howard (and Robert A.) branch of the Taft
family thus was the relatively poor one; it was the Charles
Phelps Taft side that had the important money and it is this
side that has it today. William Howard Taft, for example,
left *his* family $475,000, a quite small percentage of the
wealth of the Other Tafts.

Still, looking at this family background all in all, it is not
difficult to see that Robert A. Taft never knew some of the
disquiets that from time to time bear in upon more ordinary
men. If in his youth intellectual doubt of any kind had
crept upon him—as usually it does to inquiring young men—
then there were generations of intellectual Taft achievement,
and settled Taft conviction, to fall back upon.

If religious questions arose, then matters had been pretty
well settled when Robert Taft came upon the scene. There
had been Unitarians in the Taft family but in his time the
Tafts were for the most part of the Episcopal Church. Robert
Taft, though a reasonably active man in a religious way, was
no mystic and he had, by the way, a genuine and complete
religious tolerance. Some of his personal characteristics
varied; this characteristic never.

And as to politics, he had a career clearly marked out for
him in one way or another. Like the Roosevelts in New York
—both the Hyde Park, or Franklin Roosevelts, and the
Oyster Bay, or Theodore Roosevelts—it was only right and
proper in Ohio for him to have political preferment. The fact

that he went down with Mr. Hoover in 1932 did not diminish his ultimate prospects in the least; in Ohio a Taft can afford to lose. Other men have not so easily survived other repudiations.

And in the intimately personal way, Robert Taft had the assurance that long-inherited place in life can bring to most any man. Socially, he was at the top and he never gave that business much thought for himself, though he *was* thoughtful of others. A few years ago, at a coming-out party at the F Street Club in Washington for the debutante daughter of Doris Fleeson, the distinguished liberal columnist who had given him many a hard lick, Taft turned up to mingle bravely with a guest list most of whose members regarded him as a political dinosaur. It was engaging to watch this scene. There was Taft, sitting by himself at a table, looking with shy, myopic wonder at this curious breed, sipping his highball doubtfully but loyally sticking it out because of his friendship with Miss Fleeson. And there was the political outer breed, noticeably ignoring Taft.

The background of profound assurance—financial, intellectual, social and moral—was perhaps more complex in Taft's case than in the case of any other public man known to this generation.

The security it gave him helped him, of course, but it also did him harm. Though it was absolutely essential in the Taft family of his earlier years to do things for oneself—and still is in that family—it is nevertheless a fact that never in his life did he know economic distress or even a severe economic pinch. Able as he was, he no doubt would have made out well in any case; still this was a blank spot in his experience.

The Great Depression in our time did not mean, even faintly, to him what it meant personally to so many millions of others. The adage of the unconquerable quality of thrift and industry that had come distantly to the Taft family from New England was to him not a relative matter, but as absolute as the carving on a family tombstone.

He never lacked sympathy—for what he could understand. Years ago, when he was still active at Taft, Stettinius and Hollister in Cincinnati, he was a most considerate employer in what has always seemed, to an outsider at least, a hard profession for the young. A certain lawyer in Cincinnati, now well established, began his career under Taft. He tried a complicated lawsuit for Taft's firm and in its course his judgment was challenged by an important client in an important way. The young lawyer was losing the argument until Taft intervened. "If you don't care to follow my judgment," he snapped at the client, "then of course you must get another general counsel."

The client submitted; the epilogue was that when the junior hesitantly proposed what his fee should be, Taft announced nasally, "Not at all adequate," and raised the estimate substantially.

But these were matters he understood. Life never prepared him for a perception of the thin margin on which most of his fellow men must operate. It was a margin the nature of which he never really knew. Another inheritor of security,

Franklin Roosevelt, knew, or sensed, or was told of, this margin and this circumstance enabled him to illuminate (or to exploit, if one chooses) the story of the common man. Taft, so far as one could gather from him, always believed that this instinct, coming from Mr. Roosevelt, was synthetic, or worse. Taft imagined that he understood the common man "perfectly well"—one of his favorite phrases. He never understood him at all.

For Taft's understanding of man's troubles was personal and limited to the narrow focus of his own acquaintanceship. His years in Cincinnati did not develop that focus, except in a rather academic sense. His life elsewhere did little to expand it.

Again, circumstances caused him to miss much that is common to men. Though he plainly had a childhood that was more than satisfactory there is good ground to suspect that his relationship to his father, William Howard Taft, lacked some things in the way of understanding. Indeed, the personal differences between these two—the laughingly gregarious father and the son looking warily on anything past the second martini—can be illustrated in a small way by this single fact. The father in his drinking days had what used to be called a very strong head for alcohol; the son did not, and knew it.

The most authoritative information available indicates that while Robert Taft loved and greatly honored his father he was far from the ancestor worshiper that he has sometimes been pictured. There was, for instance, much talk in Washington after the death in 1953 of Chief Justice Fred M.

Vinson that had Bob Taft been alive he would have been offered the post by President Eisenhower. Some who knew Taft rather well believe that he would have accepted the Chief Justiceship if tendered, if only because his father had ended his career there after leaving the White House.

This is not the opinion of others who are in perhaps better position to know. Taft, by the evidence of members of his family, had no great interest in the bench and never thought of anything in the way of a family succession to the high court. It is betraying no secret (and is not intended to be gratuitous) to say, moreover, that he held some of the members of the present court in less than the highest regard and would not have gone out of his way to serve with them.

Apart from a beginning that was far from typical, Taft, again by circumstance, lost much that was within the ordinary experience of his generation. Because of nearsightedness, possibly the result of reading so many books for so many years, he was rejected for military service in the First World War. Though his service with Mr. Hoover in the relief administration in Europe brought him decorations from the governments of Poland, Finland and Belgium, he never, of course, knew combat and thus never knew war. Nobody ever questioned his courage; this would have been an absurdity and, to those few who knew the moving gallantry of his last days, almost an obscenity.

Nevertheless, it is entirely probable that his somewhat parsimonious attitude toward military preparation, and his rather wistful belief that most of it could somehow be done without, came from the fact that the indispensability of weapons was not in his *personal* knowledge.

And in him there was a long, strange and quietly dramatic war between East and Midwest. There are members of the Taft family who still use the term "Easterner" as a kind of minced epithet—and understandably, no doubt, because they thought "The East" had always dealt unfairly with the Senator. In Taft's own case, "Easterner" was at times the equivalent of "New Dealer," and sometimes he tended with an angry illogic to talk as though the two were necessarily one.

All this notwithstanding, he did spend some of the most important of his youthful years in the East and his college years, especially those at Yale, made a mark upon him that was always there, no matter how infrequently shown. It turned out that his natural companions—natural in the sense of more or less equal early educational and social bias—were almost always his opponents and sometimes his bitter antagonists.

He made his ordinary way, therefore, among men who, in a way, left him feeling very lonely. He served on the Yale Corporation with Dean Acheson, for example, but his day-by-day associates were mainly men like the late Senator Kenneth Wherry of Nebraska and Senator Eugene D. Millikin of Colorado. He had an Eastern link in the personal sense with Senator Alexander Smith of New Jersey and Princeton but the bond here, while affectionate, was not especially strong politically.

Taft knew the East in a sense that most of his midwestern associates never did. He was, in consequence, never prepared to go all the way with them in their strictures against the East—except, as was not too infrequent, when he was angry. And, on the other hand, he of course knew the Midwest as few Easterners ever did.

He was often, therefore, in a rather defensive state about one region or the other in turn, though politically he always sided in the end with the Midwest, both by predilection and conviction and a type of political necessity. He deeply resented what he considered to be an Eastern attitude of superciliousness, particularly in the intellectual and political sense, toward the Middle West. He knew his political history very well and he knew that a Republican party without the full support of the Midwest (privately he probably would have said without the *dominance* of the Midwest) would be like an army without infantry to do the hard and heavy work.

This recognition, and not altogether his own Ohio roots, made him unwilling sometimes to recognize what seemed to be the fair claims of the Republican East. That region provoked him in a variety of ways and most of all because it seemed to him to be continually nurturing so many Republicans of doubtful faith. The Roosevelt Administration, as he saw it, was uncomfortably full of these deserters; and the Truman Administration was, if anything, worse.

The Easterners, on their side, never did much to reassure him or to attempt to capture him, in whole or in part. For the most, they developed an inexact concept of him as a man

inexorably determined always to look upon the Ohio River
as at least as important as the Rhine and to regard western
Pennsylvania as the farthermost defensible outpost of the
Republican party.

Taft, for his part, was nearly always trying to break out of
a framework in which he thought he had been incontinently
and arbitrarily cast. Nearly always, he was trying to say in
a polite, low-register way that he really had, if given a
proper chance, no purely Midwestern habit and view of
life.

He never succeeded wholly, or even very substantially, in
this, in part because he was a basically intransigent man and
in part because he became a victim of a national habit of
insistently classifying men in all sorts of ways, including the
geographical. Because he was a victim of this, he had a good
deal of wry sympathy for the Southern politicians, the more
philosophic of whom have long since learned to accept with
such grace as is possible the immovable fact that they are
going to be pigeonholed willy-nilly by most of the rest of
the country.

Taft, indeed had just enough of the East in him not to be
wholly satisfied with everything about the Middle West
and quite enough of the Midwest in him to take an unduly
suspicious view at times of what was going on or might be
going on in the East. If it seems that he made altogether too
much of this geographic division it must be recalled that
when an attitude of mind lodged in him it took a good deal
to dislodge it.

Some of this unquestionably was fed by Midwestern associates, whose fundamental suspicions went far beyond those of Taft, which, while lively, were by no means always in the forefront of his consciousness.

In short, Cincinnati; the Taft family saga with all its massive strength; the family base in the Midwest with its aspect of a political Gibraltar—all these gave him an irreducible rock of security. The fact is, they all made him possible. But it may be, too, that for all their shelter they cast troubles upon him in his political life that need not have come.

4

TAFT AND THE CONSTITUTION

An old Ohio early-days political associate of Robert A. Taft was illustrating this point with his hands. "Now," he said, "suppose that something new came along in the way of legislation. Bob Taft would take that bill in this hand and in the other hand he would take the Constitution. He would have his pencil there. He would look at everything in that bill and then he would look at the Constitution. Everything in that bill had to be square with that Constitution— and I mean damn square, with no possible doubt about it at all. If it didn't, it was out; I don't care who wanted the bill, whether Bob's people or other people. That is just the way he was."

In all of government Taft, at bottom, really trusted only the written Constitution. The care and preservation of that Constitution he entrusted first to Congress, second to the courts, and last to the Presidency. As a practical matter, he put Congress first, in my understanding, for several interesting reasons. In the first place, the fact that only Congress could initiate a Constitutional amendment—and only by a two-thirds vote, at that—was always in his awareness of the properly established scheme of things. It seemed fitting to him that first responsibility should lie here, too.

In the second place, he regarded Congress, all things considered, as "safer" in Constitutional matters, and primarily because of the Senate. (He would not have cared much, I think, to serve in the turbulent House of Representatives, in whatever lofty position or on whatever terms.)

The whole structure of the Senate—its staggered terms, the fact that never are more than a third of the members up for election in any given year, the fact that individual power there does not rest on the number of voters represented—appealed to him in this regard. He had no objection, of course, to the vast popular elections that determine who is to be President.

But he had the greatest satisfaction in the arrangement by which any Senate, or even a resolute minority of Senators who might represent states with an aggregate population of one-twentieth the national population, can block any amount of popular will when it comes to altering, or "tinkering with," the Constitution. He was aware of the fact that any President can be put under far more instantaneous and effective popular pressure than can any Senate. So he thought the White House not the best place to defend the Constitution.

As to the courts, his reverence for them (in what he considered the right hands) could not have been higher. He put them second in the matter of preserving his notion of Constitutional government only because Congress had to be first.

As to the Presidency, he thought of it as properly an administrative and magisterial office, and not primarily and properly a creative one. (How he would have defined the proper scope of Presidential power had he reached that office can, of course, only be speculated upon. It is the guess of some who knew him well that, confronted with all the vast responsibilities of the White House he would have changed his mind. When he was leading the Republican cannonading at President Truman for breaking General of the Army Douglas MacArthur as Far East Commander, Taft was asked how *he* would have proceeded, as President, in such a situation. "I would have called my commander in and consulted him, I suppose," he said, "if there had been a disagreement in policy." He had the grace and sense and humor to smile at this highly improbable picture of Taft *negotiating* a policy disagreement with a subordinate.)

The Constitution to Taft was a written document in the most literal possible sense of that term; of the notion that it was a growing thing he took a pretty dim view. Accordingly, all his political life he followed what is called the narrow or rigid interpretation of the Constitution. If it said such and such at the close of the eighteenth century then, in Taft's view, it would say only precisely the same thing at the middle of the twentieth century. There can be no doubt, for instance, that the angry clamors he raised so persistently against many of the activities of the Roosevelt and Truman Administrations were not simply partisan and not solely based in his dislike of the meaning of those activities in themselves.

He was genuinely in fear lest illicit alterations be made to the Constitution under cover of the general noise of reform.

The merest suggestion, from whatever quarter, that something legislative upon which he himself had set out might not square with the Constitution was enough to frost his enthusiasm and send him on hurriedly to his law books to recheck his position.

"The whole trouble with the New Dealers," he said in one of his characteristic speeches on this point, "is that they believe that whatever they desire the [Supreme] Court should hold to be Constitutional. They do not care what happens to the fundamental principles on which this country was founded. Most of them would be willing to abolish the States and turn over all local government to Federal control. All of them favor the delegation of legislative power to the President and seem to forget that this was the first step in the growth of autocracy in Germany and Italy."

To propose that some admittedly dubious enactment be carried out by Congress so that the courts themselves could say yea or nay on Constitutional grounds was to him to propose the unthinkable. He considered such a notion to be unforgivably frivolous, appallingly reckless and dangerous and a default of Congressional responsibilities.

Thus when in 1946 he took an action that brought him a most unusual reward, the cheers of organized labor and of liberal people generally, he was saluted by most of them for the wrong reason. In May of that year the railroad unions were on strike and the country was approaching paralysis. President Harry S. Truman, new to office and then not entirely out of the grace of the nation's conservatives, asked Congress to pass a bill giving him power to draft the strikers and thus to command them to work as their Commander in Chief.

The House approved this extraordinary bill with what can fairly be called a grotesque parody on debate—incidentally giving Taft another reason, as he saw it, not to hold that honorable body in too lofty a regard. He rose in the Senate to stop the bill—to stop "this nonsense," as he put it in private —and it was in fact stopped when the Senate then took time to think it over.

It is rarely recalled that Taft did not stand wholly alone at this barricade. Waiting to fight the bill also—and willing to filibuster it, if it came to that, as was Taft himself—was a most unlikely and unchosen companion, the then left-wing Democratic Senator from Florida, Claude Pepper. No odder pair could have been found; but there it was: Taft the right-winger and Pepper the left-winger and between them drawing what to the second was commonplace and to the first quite incredible, the huzzahs of the labor unions.

Nevertheless it was primarily a Taft show (he was by this time the most powerful figure in the Senate) as he stood there in the Senate arguing his case with a mixture of scorn, irritation and impatience.

"I am not willing," he said, "to vote for a measure which provides that the President may be a dictator. It offends not only the Constitution, but every basic principle for which the American Republic was established. Strikes cannot be prohibited without interfering with the basic freedom essential to our form of Government." His use of the word "prohibited" was fortunate for his later peace of mind. He later restored the labor injunction, which can halt strikes in their progress though perhaps not quite "prohibit" them, in the Taft-Hartley labor act.

All this rather dazed some of the orthodox Taft Republicans of the country; but, as always with "Bob," they could rationalize it and then forget the incident to the extent that it did not comport with their legend of Taft. After all, or so they reasoned, Taft had taken a successful action against Truman and while it had incidentally benefited the labor unions Bob no doubt knew what he was about.

To Taft, however, it was strictly a Constitutional issue and the praise thrust upon him from so many improbable liberal quarters did not turn his head. He looked, rather, with a moody skepticism upon the kudos from these sources. While it did not exclude the Bill of Rights, his view toward the Constitution came down, at last, and fully consciously or not, to focus on the features in it that promote order and protect personal property.

He had all the traditional conservative's concern for property as an institution, because he knew it promoted privacy and freedom and he also had a greater than average politician's distrust of "the military," sometimes a quite excessive one from any point of view. The railroad strikers draft bill, therefore, offended him in the most exquisite way in relatively minor as well as major points. It offended him as an impertinence because Mr. Truman had offered it—though this is not to say that his fundamental objections would have been altered, whatever the authorship.

It offended him because of its military color. But finally

and most of all it offended him because it was, as he viewed it, an unconstitutional deprivation of an aspect of private property; that is, free enterprise and in this case the free enterprise of the strikers. The strike he detested; and the strikers he wholly deplored. But the principle he loved.

A similar reasoning was at the heart of the enormously tactless position he took in October of 1946 about the trials of war criminals in Hitler Germany and in Japan. In a speech titled "Equal Justice Under Law," which is the motto cut in stone across the face of the Supreme Court building, Taft put forward this argument:

"I believe that most Americans view with discomfort the war trials which have just been concluded in Germany and are proceeding in Japan. They violate the fundamental principle of American law that a man cannot be tried under an *ex post facto* statute.

"The trial of the vanquished by the victors cannot be impartial no matter how hedged about with the forms of justice. I question whether the hanging of those who, however despicable, were the leaders of the German people, will ever discourage the making of aggressive war, for no one makes aggressive war unless he expects to win. About this whole judgment there is the spirit of vengeance, and vengeance is seldom justice."

It is not necessary to endorse the tepidity of Taft's epithet for these outright murderers amongst the Nazis—these "despicable" men, as he chose to call them—to see him in this episode as a genuine, honest-to-God strict Constitutionalist of rare vintage (if perhaps a slightly frozen one). One must remember that to him atrocities were far away and read about; they had not fallen under his *personal* eye. None of this detracts from the extraordinary courage of his statement at the time it was made. These, the times of 1946, were the times when people still remembered who the enemy had been and what he had done and the stain of the Buchenwalds that will not for many a century be wiped out.

What Taft was saying here was, in his view, a defense of orderly and Constitutional government (the one in his mind was more or less always merged with the other) and he was thunderstruck at the vehemence with which the American skies of 1946 broke in criticism of his speech. He said what others of more judicial mind (his mind was of a judicial cast only on and off, and mostly off) were thinking but dared not say.

He was, of course, not to the faintest degree concerned with whatever severities might be handed out to the Nazi criminals themselves. What he feared here was that an *American* judicial system was taking the lead in this odd kind of prosecution, and who knew to what Constitutional damages it might lead? The approach, moreover, had for him the great defect of novelty; he did not as a rule care for novelty in any field, quite apart from the high field of the Constitution. Nor did he relish dramatic solutions of anything. He once complained, on this point, that the New Dealers had "discovered the secret of perpetual emotion." And with this modest epigram he was more than pleased.

Constitutionalism, as Taft looked at it, led him into curious byways. He was long interested in such matters as public housing and even in the tricky concept of Federal aid to local public education, a daring business which some far more liberal politicians liked to leave severely alone. He was able to sanction and even promote such innovations (though his interest declined a bit in his latter years) because he did not consider them to be anti-Constitution and because he took what can only be called a special view of certain things.

In the Taft family tradition, children, the home, the hearth, the rooftree, take a very great and compelling place—as Senator Taft's touching and open devotion to his invalid wife, Martha, whose wheel chair he himself pushed about on every possible occasion, would perhaps alone attest. But there was more to it than this. Taft in his mind severely divided the young from the adult, in every sense and in every way. To put it in a perhaps slightly oversimplified way, he thought that men should be on their own but that children should not, in any sense. Moreover, to him the protection of the young meant the protection of the home and the sufficiently stable sort of home meant the protection of the Constitution, which was the highest earthly symbol.

Therefore, he could stand resentfully skeptical of such fairly well-established things as the excess profits tax and at the same time urge that Washington, of all places, build homes at public expense in certain circumstances and even put its highly dubious hands, if ever so slightly, into the public school system. Always, he was prepared, when it came down to hard cases, to extend Federal aid to unemployed adults, but this with him was a kind of wincing charity. But always he was prepared, quite short of any situation of desperate need, to do a great deal at public expense for children. Once in a quiet conversation of a late afternoon I asked him how he could be so "conservative" in so many fields and so "liberal" in one. His reply was long, and often elliptical, and I can recall for the most part only its sense. It was to this effect: Responsibility went only with free will and children had not, of course, willed themselves here. They could, therefore, be considered as irresponsibles—in the kindest meaning of that term. They were entitled, not as a matter of privilege but as a matter of right, to a decent roof, decent meals, decent medical care and a decent place in which to go to school. The rest, as they grew older, was up to them.

And specifically as to why he could oppose the excess profits tax and support Federal aid to education, he observed with a small grin: "Education is socialistic anyhow, and has been for a hundred and fifty years." The impression was that he was using the word "socialistic" in its nonforensic sense; he did not intend "socialistic" to mean what he did when he flung the term so often at the Democrats. He meant, or so it seemed at the time, that public education was what might be called Constitutionally socialistic, much as was running the post office, and since this sort of thing was hallowed by time and had been accepted from the beginning there was no use in fearing it now.

And in the Constitutional sense Taft's most notable departure on a detail of Constitutional policy from Herbert Hoover was over Prohibition. Mr. Hoover, of course, took an essentially "dry" position. Taft, for his part, thought that Prohibition was an invasion of personal privacy and an evasion of personal responsibility and therefore an essentially unconstitutional step itself. Too, it would not have been in his character to be one of those phenomena of the Prohibition era, the "Drinking Drys."

"Meddling" was one of his favorite charges against the New Deal, as it was against the Fair Deal, and "meddling" was not only inherent in Prohibition but, as he saw it, in a dozen much later exertions and services of the Government. To give the well-remembered flavor of Taft on these meddlings—all of which he saw as frontal or oblique attacks on the Constitution—one can recall this excerpt from a Taft speech of 1944:

"Today, the Government has become a busybody, determined to meddle with everybody else's business, to regulate every detail of private enterprise and even in many cases to set in motion direct Government competition with private enterprise. Like every meddler, it has left its own proper business in complete confusion."

"There is hardly a field of activity," he went on sadly, "into which the Government has not intruded itself."

So this was Taft the Constitutionalist, sure in his own mind, at least, of his consistency, because in his own mind all that he did and planned was first of all in support of the Constitution. Right-wing views on fiscal matters and (incredible or not) often left-wing views on social matters—this was the point he reached.

Again, when it came to Taft on things like Federal aid to education, the old Taftites about the country found the intellectual going a little hard and there were even stories in the late forties of old gentlemen grumbling in their clubs: "Taft is becoming a damn Socialist." These real or legendary complaints—I never found a confirmed instance where one was known actually to have been uttered—amused Taft in the sense that two old Washington aphorisms amused him.

One of these was that Taft had "the best eighteenth-century mind in America." The other ran: "Taft has the best mind in the Senate—until he makes it up."

II.

TAFT IN RESPONSIBILITY
AND IRRESPONSIBILITY

☆ 5 ☆

ONSET OF THE POWER
AND THE GLORY

It was the Congressional elections of 1946 and the circumstance that he was already the leading "conservative" in Congress—though this term meant different things to different people—that brought Robert A. Taft to the first of his peaks of extraordinary power in this country. The Democrats approached the November test in great and justified anxiety. Rather as they had done after the exertions of the First World War, the people had got sick of sacrifice and particularly in little things like the shortage in, and high cost of, meat.

President Harry S. Truman, accompanied by Sam Rayburn of Texas, then Speaker of the House, correctly sensed the mood as one of nostalgia and weariness with wartime controls. In going home to Independence, Missouri, to vote, the President turned away from his customary jaunty means of travel. He left his airplane *The Sacred Cow* in Washington.

Sedately, and in every possible way showing his soberness of purpose, Mr. Truman went out to Independence in an old-fashioned train, while Taft was on the stump, as he always was in a time of test for his party, carrying his harsh, dedicated, dryly intolerant attack on the Democrats forward to

the very end. Taft knew, this time, what both Mr. Truman
and Rayburn knew; the Democrats were in for a very heavy
defeat. Rayburn and Mr. Truman were gloomy as they sat in
the last car of the Presidential train. Rayburn told a friend
with bitterness: "This is going to be a damn *beefsteak* election."

Nothing could better have suited Taft's book. He had made
a tireless record of attacking the then control agency, the
Office of Price Administration, raising his old jeremiad that
it was interfering with free enterprise.

The election, of course, gave the Republicans control of
all of Congress for the first time since 1928. While it could
not be said that Taft had won the election for them, it was
quite plain that he had spoken, if in a more idealistic way,
for some of the thoughts at the time of a majority of the
people. He himself was not up that year; he spoke for the
Party.

Taft, as a political classicist, took the result precisely on its
face. Though he understood and rather deplored in an
academic way the occasional pull of the small issues—in this
case the scarcity and high price of steaks—it was inconceivable to him that elections could be settled on such petty
issues alone. He supposed, as in his own case, that the people
had seen the steak situation as the mere small symbol of
what he himself thought to be wrong with the country—that
is, nearly all the accumulated policies of the Democrats.

And this was, incidentally, one of the grave shortcomings,
or instances of imperception, of his whole political career.
He never could grasp to what extent men reacted far more

trivially or emotionally than perhaps ideally they should. He had, for example, a fixed belief that highly expert discussions of, say, the philosophy of the excise tax, were to ordinary men if not enthralling at least of a considerable interest.

He had the same belief that men generally understood and accepted all the implications of their decisions. He used to argue with vehemence, for instance, that it would be no more difficult to get two-thirds of all the Senate, or sixty-four members, to sign a petition to break a filibuster than it would be to get two-thirds of a quorum, or thirty-three Senators. Because it would have been for him quite out of the question to discreetly absent himself on such an occasion he persisted in assuming, in the face of all the evidence, that this would be true of others.

Accordingly, Taft returned to Washington in 1947 from the 1946 elections sure that the popular mandate was to cast out a great many chapters of the New Deal, if not the whole book. He returned a hero, but he returned also in what was for him a fairly mellow mood, basically determined though he was. Whether one agreed with a single one of his policies he was always in the personal sense a good winner (and an even better loser) just as he was basically a good *man*, whether or not he would have been a good President.

Back in the Senate, as chairman of the Republican Policy Committee and thus in this case the party's intellectual and practical head, he was for the first time since he had reached the Senate in a position of responsibility consistent with his already large and growing power. The Republican floor leader was nominally Senator Wallace White of Maine, a

charming but not very forceful man who sat in the leader's
chair in the first row but looked openly back to Taft, a dozen
rows behind, for all the important signals.

This was a great hour for Taft. He now had in his hands, so
he felt, the *power*, since his party now had control, to trans-
form into action the millions of words of complaint and
caveat with which the orthodox Republicans, himself included, had so long showered the public and official prints.
The cast of matters was otherwise favorable, too, or so it
seemed.

The Democrats, in their long shelter from the sting of
defeat, had without a doubt got not only a little fat, as they
were in a political sense, but a little soft as well. They were
thrown into somewhat irrational panic by what had happened in November of 1946. Moreover, Taft had always been
"well connected," as they say in the South, in a political way
with many Southern Democrats in Congress, some of whom
were in highly critical positions as senior minority members
of powerful legislative committees.

Between these two principalities—that is the Taft principality among the Republicans and the Southern Democratic
principality—there had already been, in many matters, a
silent partnership, as both struck such blows as they could at
the Truman regime. Taft in 1947 began carefully to expand
this alliance. The relationship, that between Taft and the
dissident Southern Democrats, was already being at once
oversimplified and underestimated.

The Southerners, for the most part, were not really and
simply rebel party assassins lying in wait for Mr. Truman out

of a perverse and Bourbon hatred. In varying degrees of good faith, depending on the basic character of individuals, they were genuinely in fear, as was Taft, of what had been going forward in Government. And their concern was not, as often it was understated to be, simply with the Truman compulsory civil rights program, toward most of which Taft took a position of sufficient hostility.

They had joined Taft because they felt that in a great many matters—and these nearly all came down in the end to fiscal matters—he was "safer" than any Democrat who might conceivably occupy the White House for a long time to come. It was therefore a fact that while by ordinary standards they were clearly disloyal to the Democratic party as a national institution and would not for a moment have survived in a more disciplined party, they were not Taft's mere creatures nor he their master.

Mainly, he got along with them not only for such concrete reasons as mutually sympathetic views on many questions but for certain less palpable reasons as well. He was, as was each of their more important men, a parliamentarian of very high skill and a genuine lover of the parliamentary life, as a way of life. Moreover, he was a traditionalist (this was very good, to the Southerners), he was well born, his father, William Howard Taft, had been pro-Southern, and he was a highly reliable ally in a pinch.

There is no instance known to me in all his days in the Senate where Taft let down an associate in any agreed enterprise, no matter how sticky the going might have become. In these days, too, he was careful never to hit the Southerners unnecessarily at the place it would really hurt—that is, in their essential faith in an internationalism that most of the time he rejected. He tried, back in the late forties, to leave *that* subject pretty well alone.

With the Southerners often operating for him along his flank as a sort of guerrilla band to harass the regular, or Truman, Democrats, Taft formed a strong front in this, Mr. Truman's despised "worst" Eightieth Congress. He was able to bring about him, in degrees of acceptance ranging from the glad to the hesitantly willing, nearly all the Republicans— even Senator Wayne Morse of Oregon, sometimes.

Personally, as well as in the collective sense, Taft was operating in precisely the forum and in precisely the circumstances that he liked the most. He was the real leader of the Republicans in the Senate, without having to do all the dreary chores—constant attendance, constant watchfulness over the routine actions of the Democrats across the aisle, moving at the proper time to adjourn, and so on. All this was loyally done for him by Senator White.

Taft sat in a special place. From the policy committee, he commanded the action, but in what he considered a suitably distant way. For the Republicans he was like the Commanding General at Supreme Headquarters; one might not always see him, but his power was there.

The policy committee became famous, where it had been rather pedestrian before. After each of its meetings, in which rarely was anything so binding as an actual vote on policy taken, Taft was careful to announce that it was his "impression" that this or that had been "the general view" of the session. This unexpected regard for the sensibilities of other Senators (which did not come naturally, ever, to Taft) fooled nobody. It became, and pretty correctly so, the custom to consider Taft *as* the policy committee. He complained once to a friend: "I cannot open my mouth as an individual Senator without having the reporters write that 'the Republicans' have decided so and so. I have tried to point out that sometimes I am talking as one Senator; but I don't like to go on being a bore by always making that qualification."

"Don't be a bore any more, then," said the friend. Taft smiled.

Though he had the highest, proprietary interest in the important things that went on, it was very hard for him in those days to stomach a good deal of what was said on the floor. Almost literally he detested time-wasting and almost literally he hated what he considered to be nonsense.

There were times, when the business at hand seemed to him to be trivial and worse, that he would shake his head for all to see; first sadly and then vigorously and in open anger as it all droned on. Occasionally moved to uncontrollable exasperation, he would rise, glare all about him and stalk from the chamber into the Republican lounge. He would certainly have slammed the door, except that it operates without noise.

Shortly, calmed and rested, he would return with an air of resignation and sit out the rest of the session. He had an extraordinary loyalty from his Republican associates, considering the fact that he sometimes made it clear in the plainest and most public way that he regarded one or another of them as a dolt. In this, the fact that he never gladly suffered a man he considered a fool, he was absolutely nonpartisan. The offenders, in his eyes, were as often Republicans as Democrats—a little more often, if anything.

When there occurred an offense of this sort, that is, an assault upon his common sense, it could bring from Taft a rare burst of profanity (he was ordinarily a prim-speaking man) even up to a sharp, very rare, "Goddamn." When fellow Republican Senators called upon him in his office to propose this or that he would hear any suggestion at any time but if he thought it foolish or impractical he would say so, and at once. Rarely has a man been forgiven so much by so many; but forgive him they did, perhaps because the Republican sense of hierarchy is much stronger than that of the Democrats and because Taft was the hierarch.

He never spoke, so far as can be found, in such a way, in any circumstances, to a subordinate or to a member of his office staff. He might look quite pained and long-suffering; but then he would let it go at that. No man I ever knew in politics had greater devotion from his staff, the members of which really considered him selfless and knew him to be fundamentally kind.

It was this man, with all his strength and all his weakness, who came to typify the Eightieth Congress, a type figure that President Truman was at pains to use very often when he spoke of that Congress.

Taft's function, as he saw it, was not only to make a *Republican* record but, though in a less imperative sense, to make a record on which he himself would again stand for the Presidential nomination. As it turned out, the Republican record he made—which had at minimum the virtue of candor —probably defeated the Republicans in 1948 and elected President Truman to his first full term in the White House. And it flung over Taft the shadow that never left him—"*He can't win.*"

For the Midwestern Republicans, of whom he was in so many ways the personification, lost control of and touch with Taft at the single point where they were themselves more relatively liberal—that is, in the area of farm subsidies. Taft on this issue merged with the little group of extreme right-wing Eastern Republicans, who were as powerful in the House of Representatives as they were powerless in the country. These had no stomach in principle for Government payments to farmers, as they had no stomach for any other sort of Government intervention in "free enterprise."

The immediate result was that the Republican Eightieth Congress, with Taft as leader and symbol, reduced the money available to the Commodity Credit Corporation. This meant that fewer cribs could be built to store the surplus grain in the farm belt and this meant heavy selling at comparatively "distressed" prices because without storage places one could not get a Government "loan" on his corn and wheat.

The consequent wrath of the farmers is now a part of the country's recent political history. President Truman, speaking of the record of the Eightieth Congress in Iowa in the campaign of 1948, declared that the Republicans had "stuck a pitchfork in the farmer's back." Even Taft's Ohio went Democratic that year.

That Taft himself was fully aware in advance of the implications of the corn-crib bill is doubtful; even if he had been I believe he would have pressed on as he did. All through his career he opposed in principle, or at least cut down, these subsidies all that he could. Once, he journeyed to Nebraska in the heart of the farm belt and in the Republican heartland as well, to announce with harsh, casual candor that farm prices were too high.

In the spring of 1953 he told a group of Ohio farm leaders in Washington that he hoped the Eisenhower Administration's then developing farm program would appeal, as he put it, to their "intellects." In Cleveland, at a meeting of a soil conservation district (for soil conservation the farmer gets many Federal benefits) he said that he was "tired of seeing all these people riding around in Cadillacs."

No other Midwestern politician would have remotely dared to utter such wounding heresies, though many of them on balance were well to the right of him. How the Midwest rationalized *this* side of Taft cannot be rationally explained. He was simply Taft and so somehow they "understood" him. And in the meantime, of course, Taft on farm subsidies was, from the point of view of such crusty old-fashioned Eastern Republicans as chose untypically to follow him, on exactly the right track.

While Taft, in this first Congress that he dominated, was allowing the alienation of the farmers, and chipping away thus at one aspect of the New Deal, he was moving powerfully in other directions to make the *Republican* record. He gave his enormous influence to the Republican tax-cutting bill in 1947, even though he looked sourly about him at all the "hot" postwar money that was floating around the country and even though here and there a genuinely Taftian kind of banker appeared in Congress to suggest that this was the time to begin to reduce that national deficit at which Taft and others had been thundering so long.

Taft took—and indeed even insisted upon—the view that one did not need to fight inflation by retaining (or even increasing) taxes, though certainly this went against a large bibliography on the subject. The "encouragement" given to business by lower taxes, he argued, would somehow do the trick. It was hard not to see in all this an uncharacteristic Taft trimming to other wills, in this case the will of business. The vast majority of business wholly outtalked the handful of glum old hard-money men who were sadly ready to take their lumps and go on paying higher taxes. And Taft went with the majority.

But then, of course, he returned in his time to the classically conservative way—and it may be, indeed, that he went along with the tax cut because he feared he could never hold his Republican followers if he came out against it. At any rate, as chairman of the Senate Labor Committee, he set out then on the masterwork of his life, the Taft-Hartley labor act.

6

TAFT-HARTLEY,
THE MASTERWORK

In 1947, when Robert A. Taft set out to revise a body of Federal labor law that had been fixed in its essentials for twelve years, the general political movement in the United States was toward the right, and to this extent, therefore, toward all that Taft here represented. The Wagner Act of 1935, so named for the late Democratic Senator Robert F. Wagner of New York, had been declared by labor leaders to be "Labor's Magna Charta," and it was politically the most significant single act of Franklin D. Roosevelt's First New Deal. Its basic purpose was to put the strongest protections about labor's right to bargain collectively—that is, to seek through unions and union action what could not be attained by men as individuals.

The years from 1935 to 1947 had, however, seen the end of a great depression, the onset and conclusion of a great war and a rising general prosperity. It seems, moreover, at this distance an objective evaluation to say that much American public opinion, and probably most of it, had reached this conclusion: Management, in the old pre-Wagner days, had become altogether too arrogant and too powerful in dealing with the employees; now organized labor had become altogether too arrogant and too powerful in dealing with the employers, and particularly with the general public. There had been, during the war, much bitter comment that *soldiers* in their foxholes did not strike. And, probably most important of all, American industry was being successfully presented in many quarters as *the* great victor in the war, though it was conceded that perhaps several hundred Allied divisions had had some part as well.

Though this view was as objectionable to ordinary good taste as were the billboards suggesting that men had gone to war to protect their "right to boo the Brooklyn Dodgers," it all reflected nevertheless a state of fact. The American people clearly did believe that the Wagner Act was no longer to be regarded as untouchable. President Truman—this, again, was in the celebrated "Bob Taft Eightieth Congress"—himself asked for a bill that would outlaw jurisdictional strikes and secondary boycotts and would require arbitration of disputes over the meaning of existing labor-management contracts.

A coal strike was in prospect and the vast union contracts in steel and other basic things were to expire within a few months. Mr. Truman, of course, did not have in mind what he later got from Congress—not by a very long chalk—but he *had* in fact, to this extent, sanctioned a reopening of the subject of labor legislation.

Senator Taft as chairman of the Senate Labor Committee was not only the holder of jurisdiction in the routine and jurisdictional sense. He was by all odds the dominant figure in a Republican Congress and he had been seized of this whole issue, so to speak, for years as he had gone his way

trying to bring down the fundamental structure of the New
Deal.

He was, in a limited sense, in a position of tactical difficulty
in the Senate; for a good many Republicans did not share
his happy view that the 1946 Congressional elections had
indicated that the Democrats necessarily were on the way
out for a long time to come. The Labor Committee over
which he presided was pro-labor all the way on the Democratic side and even as to the other side several non-Taft,
non-orthodox Republicans had crept in, or been allowed in.
There was, for example, Senator Irving M. Ives of New York,
an old associate of Governor Thomas E. Dewey and thus, by
Taft's automatic definition, a man certain to be hostile to
Taft and to his designs. Still, Senator Taft, who had the
power more or less to suggest decisively what new Senators
should go onto what committee, not only did not stop Ives'
entry to the Labor Committee but, as he once told me, actually insisted on it.

"I felt," he said in explanation, "that the Dewey side had a
right to a seat there."

Apart from Ives there were, from Taft's viewpoint, at least
two other potentially unreliable Republican committeemen—
Senators George D. Aiken of Vermont and Wayne Morse of
Oregon. Moreover, Senator H. Alexander Smith of New Jersey
could not be viewed, in advance and with certainty, as a
pillar of Taft strength. Because he believed so strongly in
order within the Republican party, and because from time
to time he did have bouts of intellectual tolerance, Taft did
not attempt to alter this somewhat forbidding prospect in

the committee by any effort to pack or to intimidate the Republican side. The Democrats, of course, he knew he would never convince or control; he therefore wasted no time on them, at any stage.

He went at his essential mission—to get rid of at least a good deal of the Wagner Act—with what was, even for him, a remarkably single-minded zeal, touched often with a private sense of irony. Though he had been for eight years a member of the Labor Committee, he was not at that time generally considered an expert in labor law—and he himself did not think that he was. He went accordingly to the place where after all he was perhaps most of all at home, the study table. He began also to consort with some rather odd characters in order to get their views—a circumstance that pained the Taftites when they began to learn how the wind was blowing.

Though one cannot, of course, prove the point in any documentary way, it seemed quite plain to detached observers at the time that some of the employing groups at the start of the Eightieth Congress were rubbing their hands in the greatest satisfaction, in the belief that when it came to dealing with labor Taft would be "safe" in the most absolute sense of that term.

But, as was to happen so often in Taft's career, what they knew about the man was far less than what they did not. Though committed to the opinion that organized labor had got hold of far too much power, and though setting out here as elsewhere to make both for the Republican party and for himself a Taft record, Taft did not approach this matter with a lack of objectivity. The truth is that apart from all the political considerations—and these were, of course, solidly and visibly with him—he was fascinated by the problem for itself. Here were questions of high national policy intriguingly intertwined with the Constitution, with free enterprise and, last but not necessarily least, with Taft's odd social views, which, relative to those of some of his fellow orthodox Republicans, were from time to time positively dangerous.

Back of all, however, was the concept that strikes, or stoppages of manufacturing or service for any reason, were disorderly and wasteful and ought to be prevented in every way that this could be accomplished without offending Taft's sense of right and justice. Though it has been said a thousand times that Taft set out simply in a punitive frame of mind and with a spirit of vengeance (the political action committees of labor having long since made him a favorite antagonist) it is my belief that any bystander who saw the whole Taft-Hartley business unfold would not accept this charge.

Taft did not automatically exculpate management when a strike occurred; he simply disliked the whole untidy affair and sometimes he thought that management had been provocative or foolish. He profoundly grieved many among the employing groups before the Taft-Hartley issue was well in motion. Whatever views he had on the subject were his own, gathered without apparent deep bias from both sides, and any employer who thought that in Taft he was dealing with a captive could not have been more mistaken.

In the House of Representatives, to the contrary, the Truman Democrats raised rather convincing cries that representatives of employer groups, the National Association of

Manufacturers in particular, had helped to write the House version of the bill, which was in the charge of the then Representative Fred A. Hartley, Jr., a New Jersey Republican. Hartley himself once told reporters with the utmost candor that the bill on his side of the Capitol was "not a Hartley bill but a Leadership bill," meaning that he was acting for the dominant Republicans of the House.

But on the Senate side there could be no possible question about whose bill it was. It was Taft's, and when at length Congress had finished its work the result was nearly all Taft's work as well. Into this he put a particular kind of effort and what was his particular kind of brilliance—the amassing of enormous numbers of relevant and powerful facts, which he marshaled, controlled and recalled with an almost incredible virtuosity.

While it would be absurd, of course, to suppose that he had no inherent prejudices at all, the Taft-Hartley episode was, for all that, the finest example of Taft on facts. Of the many hard and bitter words that were said about him as the debate went on—including the epithet "the slave labor bill"— he said little, and that little only in a kind of absent way.

But let a factually incorrect statement be made about a factual provision and he rose in rage. A man could safely say, in short, that Taft was designing to make peons out of the American workmen. But only at his peril could he say that Taft had put in a provision for, let us say, a hundred-day "cooling off period" when this period was in fact for sixty days. One of the most extraordinary of Taft's performances was a cold denunciation of a conservative columnist and well-wisher, David Lawrence, who in an article had misstated, as Taft saw it, something or other about the bill. Taft cried out from the floor that Lawrence had written a "puerile" article.

And in this long search for, and embrace of, "the facts," Taft showed an aspect of his character that was usually hidden. As he was in a single sense a snob, that is, in the intellectual sense, he had the greatest pleasure in recognizing what he considered a good mind, to whatever purpose it might be devoted.

In covering the Taft-Hartley debate as a reporter, I had need to see Taft nearly every day, sometimes sending in a message asking him to leave the floor. He was co-operative about this, except for now and then. Curious, I asked him about these exceptions. "I won't leave the floor when Pepper [Senator Claude Pepper, Democrat of Florida] is speaking," he explained. "Fellow's able; very able; very good mind."

If a total antithesis of Taft had been sought in all of Washington, it would have been Pepper, a Fair Dealer then, who was always far out ahead of President Truman himself. It was not that Taft cared for Pepper or was afraid of his speeches; he sat to hear him in a sort of intentional professional tribute. In this one way, they belonged to the same club.

The weeks when he was making the Taft-Hartley Act disclosed to his associates more of Taft's many sides. In the Senate Labor Committee, after its hearings had been held, he went on offering "tough" proposals for the bill that he considered indispensable—and the committee, in the control of a coalition formed of the Democrats and of the liberal

Republicans, went on knocking them severally down. On nearly every ultimate provision of the bill—for example that which made coercion of employees an unfair practice by a union—he was defeated in the committee.

He took these setbacks with a philosophic resignation. His attitude was for the most part quite impersonal and almost professorial, much as though the members of a graduate seminar over which he was presiding had politely declined to accept his view of a book on economics.

When he went to the Senate floor to take his appeal from all these committee actions he reported what had occurred without rancor, was obviously on good personal terms with the Republican recalcitrants, and put it all up to the Senate with an air of saying: "Now, this *I* wanted; this is what *they* wanted. What view do you, as a whole Senate, take of this business?"

One by one the Senate restored for him all the items he had lost in the committee—all but a section that would have forbidden industry-wide bargaining, and he himself abandoned this on reflection because he knew it would have been a close thing, and the more he thought about it the less certain he was about its value anyhow.

But while he was fighting in the Senate to overturn the preliminary decisions of what he believed to be an unwarrantedly liberal labor committee, he was fighting as well to soften the much harder approach that the House was taking in the legislation. In between times he had to defeat as well a series of efforts at such an approach by individual right-wing Senators from the Senate floor.

In the end, he had his way, in both chambers. In the conference between the Senate and House to reconcile their divergent texts he wholly dominated the scene and what at length came forth was about all that he had wanted, little more and little less. Senator Aiken, a liberal Eastern Republican, described the end product as "a just bill, mild in comparison to the punishment which might be meted out to labor unions if certain extremists in the field of industry could write the bill to suit themselves."

But the Truman Democrats retorted, in the words of Senator Harley M. Kilgore of West Virginia, that a "twenty-five per cent solution of carbolic acid might be considered mild compared to a hundred per cent solution."

The vote on final passage of the Taft-Hartley bill in the House was 308 to 107 and in the Senate 68 to 24. The House overrode President Truman's veto by 331 to 83 and the Senate 68 to 25. Taft's pleasure in this latter result was momentarily diminished because his private predictions were a little off. He had expected the Senate vote to override to be the same as it had been on passage, 68 to 24.

When he first put the bill before the Senate, on April 23, 1947, he spoke not from manuscript, in spite of the largeness of the issue, but only from notes; he rarely used prepared speeches. He said that what he was after was only to "equalize" the bargaining power of labor and management. "Today," he said, "the power is all on the side of the labor leaders, except perhaps as to the very largest companies in the United States. The labor leaders have acquired a great power, which inevitably has been abused by some."

He went to the country in a radio speech on May 13, 1947, the day after the bill had first been approved by the Senate. "This bill," he declared then, "has been violently attacked by labor leaders. It has been criticized by industrialists because it does not abolish all union shops and nation-wide collective bargaining and because it does not repeal the Norris-LaGuardia Act [the Act that ended the labor injunction in the United States] except in the case of a strike affecting substantially an entire industry and threatening the national safety or health. In such cases (under the Taft-Hartley Act) injunctions may be granted only for eighty days, until mediation can be pursued and a strike vote (again) taken.

"Our committee conducted hearings for six weeks and listened to the evidence of employers, employees, labor leaders and experts in labor relations. The labor leaders simply opposed all changes in the existing law as they have opposed all attempts to reform labor abuses for the last ten years. . . . The labor ads scream loudly, without discrimination between reasonable reform and some of the proposals of extremists that are really intended to put the unions out of business.

". . . It seems to me that our aim should be to reach the point where, when an employer meets with his employees, they have substantially equal bargaining power, so that neither side feels it can make an unreasonable demand and get away with it. . . . Originally, before the passage of any of these laws, the employer undoubtedly had an advantage in dealing with his employees. He was one man; the employees might be thousands, and he could deal with them one at a time.

"Congress passed the Wagner Act in order that the employees of a single employer might act as one in dealing with the one employer in order that they might be on a sound and equal basis, a principle which I think no one can question and which certainly is not questioned in the [Taft-Hartley] bill. . . .

"The Wagner Act was enacted for a proper purpose but the result of the actual administration of that act has been completely one-sided. . . . So that today in my opinion the weight in collective bargaining is all on the side of the labor leaders except perhaps against the very largest companies of the United States. In particular I believe that in dealing with small business, with farmers and even with the workers themselves the labor union leaders have acquired a power which today the people resent and which inevitably has been abused."

The principal points in the new Taft-Hartley Act were these: The closed shop was forbidden; union shop agreements were made lawful only if a majority of all employees voted for them by secret ballot; jurisdictional strikes and secondary boycotts were made illegal; it was provided that labor unions might be sued for breach of contract; unfair labor practices for unions as well as employers were defined; it was provided that in any industry in interstate commerce there must be a sixty-day moratorium, before there could be a lawful strike; unions were required to make their financial affairs public; the eighty-day injunction was provided for in national health-and-safety strikes.

Taft was in a very high mood in those days. He was conscious that he was putting the name Taft before the country with more force than it ever had been put there before except, perhaps, by his father as President. He had the enormous personal satisfaction of carrying his bill through both houses of Congress with a bipartisan majority. And, sweetest of all to him, he achieved this same bipartisan majority in the overriding of Mr. Truman's veto.

All, to Taft, was almost perfect. He was dealing with something suitably sensible and palpable. He was taking a great responsibility—always in itself a pleasure to him. He was hitting a great blow at the New Deal; he was reaching for what he considered the jugular vein of its power, its long, intimate association with the great unions, whose own power he was going to reduce. And best of all he was restoring the country, in this field, to what he regarded as a properly *Republican* policy.

Having regard also to Mr. Truman's defeat on the tax-reduction bill, in which Congress also had overridden his veto, Taft saw the future open up as he had not seen it open before. He left the impression with his friends that while he had thought in 1940 that he *might* become President, he now was fairly certain that in good time this would come about.

Looking at the thing literally and realistically, his mind saw the position about this way: Mr. Herbert Hoover was an elder statesman, but now no more than that. As for the only part of the Republican party that really counted—that is, the orthodox Republicans whose base was in the Midwest —its only logical head was now Taft.

This was so, as Taft saw it, because the Republicans, so long out of power, had incessantly demanded that the "trend toward socialism and statism" be reversed. Others, Governor Dewey of New York among them, had talked; but Taft had acted. He had gone forward to the very hot firing line. (And this was an undoubted fact.) He had carried all the assault in Congress. (And this was an undoubted fact.) What the Republicans needed was a leader in the national sense, and this he had become. If there was any sense of logic (quite apart from any sense of justice) who but Taft could that leader be? What Taft thought then was certainly thought, moreover, by many very acute politicians, including most of the Democrats. *They* knew him as the enemy (though it is true that from Mr. Truman down their identification of Taft was the more ready because they thought he would be the easiest of all national Republicans to beat for the Presidency). Many of them genuinely believed, too, with the sometimes curiously disinterested view that one political "pro" can take of another, that Taft had in fact won his chance at "the big job."

Certainly, the Taft-Hartley achievement, if viewed only as a political fact of life, was a tremendous one. Taft, though this was not so well known, had fought off reactionary extremists on this issue almost as fiercely as he had fought off the liberal Democrats. Ordinarily a partisan Republican in the most literal sense, he had in this case actually brought along with him a majority of the Democrats against all the exertions of a Democratic President. It was the first real and major uprooting of an established New Deal policy—and in 1953, six years later, it remained the first and the last.

And, as time would indicate, this was not in fact a "slave labor bill" or anything approximating that. Clearly it became accepted by most of the people as a part of American life— not perfect but good enough to last seven years without a serious effort in Congress at its amendment in any substantial way. This, indeed, was the only major legislative accomplishment, in the affirmative sense, that in all of Robert Taft's political life was genuinely popular. It is, seen in this light, a rather sadly lonely marker in the career of "Mr. Republican"—and it was for this that he was more vehemently beaten about the head than for anything he ever did.

It marked him out as a doing and not merely a talking Republican. This, as he saw it, in a kind of frustrated awe at what to him was a wild assault on logic, was his crime in the eyes of "the Dewey people."

7

THE SAD, WORST PERIOD

The aftermath of the 1948 election, in which Governor Dewey was defeated as the Republican Presidential nominee by Harry S. Truman in one of the incredible upsets of American political history, began the worst and most melancholy period of Robert A. Taft's life as a public man. He took up, over a long time and in many ways, an attitude of a sour and embittered political frustration that was, in simple fact, unworthy of his personal tradition and beneath all that he had been—and, happily, was to be again.

All this is said entirely apart from the highly disputed *policies* that he developed and pressed in this period; what are referred to here are *personal* actions.

An uncharacteristic cynicism seemed to animate a great deal of what he did and said. Saddest of all, the Taft mind, which on the whole had an extraordinary purity of motive, whether or not its conclusions were always logically sound, seemed in this period to have clouded over with a long mood of irresponsibility that was wholly foreign to his other years.

This unfortunate period in its least attractive phases persisted from early 1949 onward, off and on, until 1952. Ironically, it spanned precisely the time when the public would otherwise have been becoming cumulatively aware of Taft's great qualities—qualities that he had a kind of genius for hiding or obscuring in his profound ineptitude for what are called human and public relations. Witness his statement in 1947, when there was a great to-do about meat prices, that people ought to "eat less."

This was, in any case, the period that had more to do with the final rejection of Taft's Presidential ambitions than any combination of external events and circumstances—probably not excepting the circumstance that a man named Eisenhower came along in 1952.

The defeat of the Republican party in Governor Dewey's campaign hit Taft an almost insupportably hard blow. Without a doubt, he suffered more than he would have had he himself been nominated and then defeated. He never could have been charged with a purely personal pettiness or a personal vindictiveness. But here was a case where his party —and how he loved it!—had been, as he saw it, let down both by the decision at the Philadelphia convention to run Dewey and then by Dewey's so-called "me too" campaign.

Taft felt to the end that he had been frozen out in the conduct of that campaign, that Governor Dewey was making no real fight against the detested Democrats and that "Trumanism" or "New Dealerism" or "Fair Dealerism"—these were all synonymous to the Senator—had in consequence been fastened upon a suffering country for the foreseeable future.

He did not begin here to blame most of the Republican party's troubles on Dewey—he had been of that mind for some time—but it was here that for Taft there hardened into an unalterable conviction what had been heretofore a strong and active suspicion. He did not campaign for Dewey with any enthusiasm and he left many of his friends with the impression that had not the *Republican party* been involved he would not greatly have cared who won as between Dewey and Truman.

Taft, with the instinct for all blacks and all whites in political action that was strangely like Truman's, cannot have been pleased even with Dewey's efforts in 1944, and particularly not with what some others thought was simply Dewey's magnanimity and sound limitation on partisanship in keeping out of certain delicate foreign policy questions in the middle of a great war.

To Taft this was a sort of negation of justified partisanship, rather a white flag. It is not ascertainable now whether he knew at the time the full reason for Governor Dewey's attitude. Mr. Cordell Hull, who was then Franklin Roosevelt's Secretary of State, has disclosed the reason. Mr. Hull, as he put it to his biographer, Harold Hinton, felt alarmed in 1944, what with the war being at crisis and the Dumbarton Oaks conference being on schedule for the autumn, that certain foreign policy matters might become involved in the Presidential campaign. He "got word" to Dewey that in his view the intrusion at such a time of such issues might be all but fatal. He asked the Governor to come to Washington for a full and frank discussion of the whole position. Dewey, as the Hull account goes, was unable himself to come but sent John Foster Dulles, who was later to become President

Eisenhower's Secretary of State. Governor Dewey, in Mr. Hull's opinion, co-operated fully and served the national interest.

But it was not in Taft's nature to approve any holiday in partisanship and in an election year, of all years. All the more was he furious in 1948 when, as he saw it, Dewey again turned the other cheek to the Democrats while Truman was making his celebrated "give 'em hell" speeches at the whistle stops about the country.

Taft watched this in growing consternation, almost in horror, much as a football coach would look at a back who went to earth before he was brought down. He told me after the election that he had known at least three weeks ahead of time that Dewey was going to lose. "I knew it for certain," he added, "when Martha told me that she could no longer listen to Dewey's speeches or watch him on the television." And he sadly informed friends early on election night, 1948, many hours before the result was becoming apparent to others, "Ohio is gone," meaning that it had gone Democratic.

Thus when Taft returned to Washington for the Eighty-first Congress, which opened in January of 1949 after the roof had so unpredictably fallen in upon the Republicans in the recent November, he returned as another Taft. He was at times almost literally beside himself. His stated view that the Democrats were literally destroying the country was not a mere forensic but a fact of his life; he meant it when he said it.

Now, he thought, the Democrats would go on with these evil designs toward an imponderable but certainly gloomy future. And apart from the fact that he was never reconciled to Dewey's defeat—not out of sympathy for Dewey but out of anguish for the party—he felt that even if the Republicans had to go down to defeat they should have gone down in his definition of fighting all the way.

What had occurred, as he saw it, was a defeat that was bad enough in itself but intolerable in what seemed to him to have been the outright rejection of Republicanism by a Republican candidate. Moreover, some of the Eastern Republicans returned to Congress, along with Taft, unconscionably inclined to blame *him* more than Dewey. As the new Congress set out upon its work, with the unhappy Republicans again thrust down into the dank minority after the brief sunshine of the Eightieth Congress, some of these Easterners attempted to organize a movement to unseat Taft as chairman of the Senate policy committee.

Though he publicly ignored this maneuver, by which it was proposed to supplant him with a Senator like Henry Cabot Lodge, Jr., of Massachusetts, it deeply wounded Taft, and this in spite of the fact that it never had a chance of success. He took what was for him the amazing action of privately thanking (in an embarrassed, diffident sort of way) some of those correspondents who wrote correctly that the rebellion had little popular base and that Taft would remain in certain control.

All this—the debacle of 1948 and the Eastern challenge to him again in early 1949—stirred him in most unfortunate ways. It seemed even to some of his friends and admirers that he began, if unconsciously, to adopt the notion that almost *any* way to defeat or discredit the Truman plans was acceptable. There was, in the intellectual sense, a blood-in-the-nostrils approach; and no mistake about it.

Thus, Taft was quoted by several reporters as having said in March, 1950, at the height of the campaign of Senator Joseph R. McCarthy alleging a Communist infiltration of the State Department, that McCarthy should "keep talking and if one case doesn't work out he should proceed with another." In a column he was writing at the time for friendly newspapers—against the coming test of his own campaign for re-election that year in Ohio—he complained that Truman had the bad habit to *"assume the innocence* of all the persons mentioned in the State Department." Again, he declared: "Whether Senator McCarthy has *legal evidence,* whether he has overstated or understated his case, is of lesser importance. The question is whether the Communist influence in the State Department *still exists."* (Emphasis mine.) This sort of thing was not the Taft that one had known; Taft the Constitutionalist, Taft the lawyer, Taft the man of privilege and education.

He seemed genuinely astonished at the outcry that arose over such of his statements as these. He said that he had been misrepresented in some regards; that the meaning of what he said was simply that McCarthy had a right to proceed in an orderly way with his cases and that President Truman, for his part, was refusing to take an objective view of the fact that Communist influence in the State Department had been charged.

What shook some of Taft's friends was not that he wanted

to support an inquiry into serious accusations against the Democrats that ought, of course, to have been seriously investigated. It was his stated view that the nature of McCarthy's evidence was not a very important consideration and his unqualified finding, long before the inquiry had ended, that Communist influence had existed, whether or not it still did.

Again, at a small dinner party in 1949 during a discussion of the then procedures of the Un-American Activities Committee of the House of Representatives one of those present said to Taft: "Senator, the committee has every right to make its investigations, but plenty of people just think some of its methods have been unfair."

"What difference does that make?" snapped Taft. "*I* am always being unfairly attacked and accused, for that matter."

This was too much for a conservative Southern Senator, an intimate Taft friend, as it was too much for most of the others present. Though it is a tricky business to presume to interpret the words of others, I am quite certain that Taft did not literally mean what he appeared to mean—that is, that unfairness was inconsequential. What he meant was that in political life the widest latitude had to be given in the area of charges and countercharges and that one must put up with this as part of the American political tradition.

What he seemed honestly not to grasp, however, was the extremely relevant fact that a Taft, with all the powerful forum of the United States Senate at his command, was far more able to take care of himself than some faceless junior bureaucrat in the State Department.

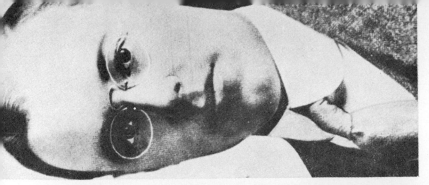
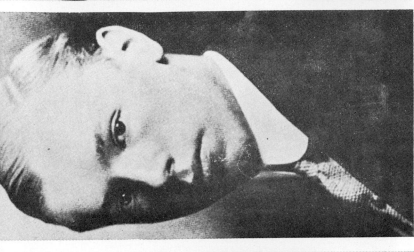

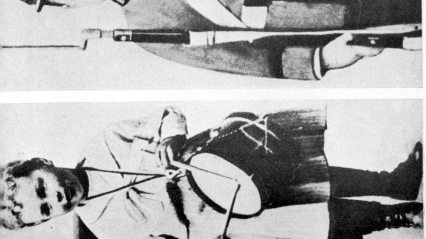

Four early pictures of Robert Taft. (Left to right) As a drummer boy at four, and in a soldier's uniform at the age of eight; a nineteen-year-old at Yale, and at thirty, while he was a member of the Ohio legislature.

(Above) A picture taken of the Taft family in 1908. Robert, then a student at Yale, with his sister, Mrs. Frederick Manning, his mother, his younger brother Charles, and his father, William Howard Taft, then President-elect of the United States. (Below) Robert Taft and Mrs. Manning with their mother in 1934.

(Left) Robert Taft during his first term in the Senate, 1938. (Right) Seeking the Republican Presidential nomination in 1940, Taft is here seen advancing his principles for a GOP program before the Republican Club of Massachusetts at the end of 1939.

Senator Taft and Senator Arthur Vandenberg in Chicago before the opening of the Republican National Convention in 1944. Mr. Taft was Chairman of the Platform Committee.

(Above) Mr. and Mrs. Taft and their sons (left to right) William, Lloyd, Horace and Robert at the Republican Convention in Philadelphia, 1948. (Below) Fellow alumni Robert Taft and Dean Acheson chat with Charles Seymour, then President of Yale, before a Washington area Yale alumni meeting in 1950.

Senator Taft and John L. Lewis converse amicably after a bitter clash during a subcommittee hearing on proposed mine safety legislation in January, 1952.

Mrs. Taft was an invaluable and tireless stumper for her husband. Here she addresses a meeting of Republican women in Seattle in 1947 while the Senator is speaking elsewhere.

A family-album picture of the Tafts on the front porch of the Taft summer home in Murray Bay, Quebec. Left to right: top row, Sean (son of William), Senator Taft, Mrs. Taft; second row, Mrs. Robert Taft, Jr., Horace Taft, Mrs. William H. Taft, Lloyd Taft, Mrs. Lloyd Taft and William H. Taft II; bottom row, Martha, Willie, Deborah, Robert III, Maria, Sarah, Virginia on mother's lap, and Louisa. Missing from the group is the fourth son of the Senator, Robert Taft, Jr.

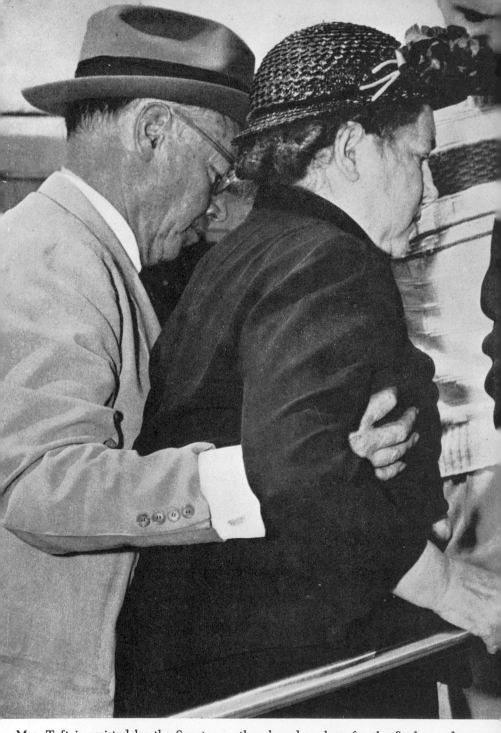

Mrs. Taft is assisted by the Senator as they board a plane for the final round of Taft's battle for the Republican Presidential nomination in 1952.

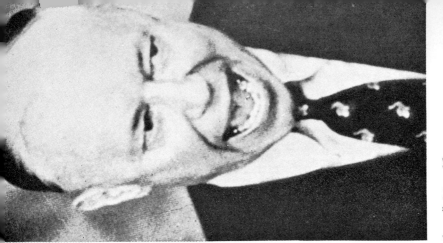

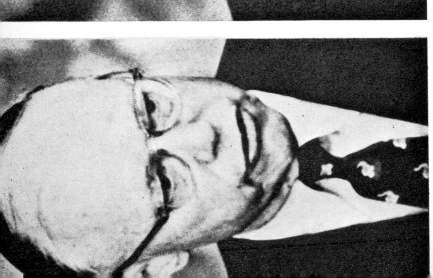

Three views of Mr. Taft during his nationally-televised "Answer to Abilene," June 19, 1952, when he blasted General Eisenhower on domestic and foreign issues.

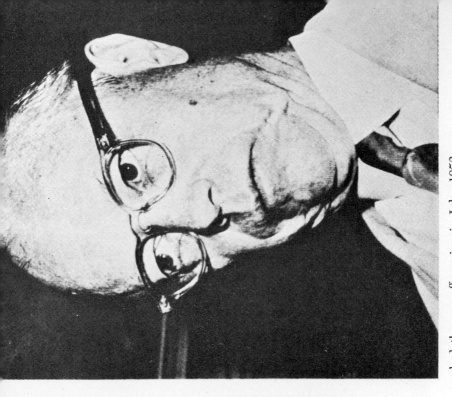

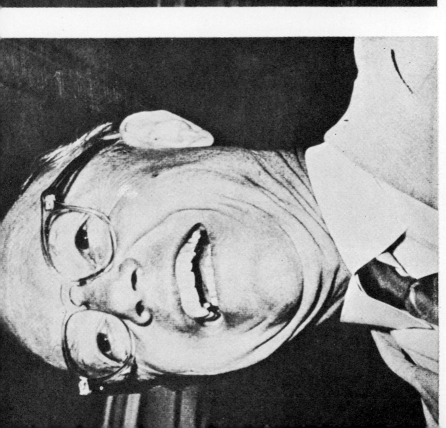

As the Republican National Convention approached the pay-off session in July, 1952, Taft alternated between gay and serious moods.

(Above) This was the scene in Chicago when General Eisenhower walked across the street to see the Senator, after winning the Republican nomination for President. (Below) Mr. Taft and General Eisenhower at their first face-to-face meeting after the convention at Eisenhower's Morningside home on September 12. Here Taft pledged his support for the General's campaign.

Here Senator Taft makes his first speech urging the election of General Eisenhower at a party rally in Springfield, Ohio, on September 17, 1952. He also supported the candidacy of his brother Charles for Governor of Ohio.

Senator Taft made a trip to Augusta, Georgia, to join President Eisenhower in a golf game in April, 1953. This picture was taken on the links of the Augusta National Country Club. It was about this time that Senator Taft became aware of the symptoms of his fatal illness.

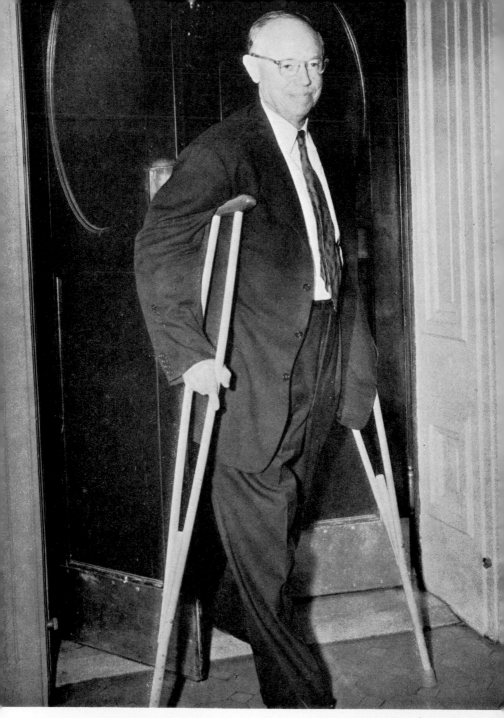

This picture was taken at the moment Senator Taft's career in the Senate ended, June 10, 1953. He walks off the Senate floor with the aid of crutches, having just turned over the floor leadership of the Republicans to William Knowland.

An honor guard stands by the bier of Senator Taft in the hushed rotunda of the nation's Capitol on August 2, 1953. Memorial rites were held the following day.

As to McCarthy, Taft's attitude could fairly be described as fundamentally pro. He said in 1952 of McCarthy's heavy primary victory in Wisconsin: "I didn't endorse him, you know, because I never interfere in other state primaries. But I did and do approve of his accomplishments in rooting out Communists and subversives in Government."

There is little doubt that Taft could have moderated McCarthy's methods, for he had McCarthy's vast admiration, but it would not be exact to attribute to Taft any direct responsibility, though certainly he had a moral one. While his power in the Senate was matchless, it still was not total; no man can utterly control another there and certainly not another who became, as did McCarthy after the 1952 election, a committee chairman. Taft's basic attitude appeared to be a pragmatism run wild. It must first of all be assumed, too, however, that he really believed that Communists were operating in the State Department, though it is hard to accept it that he really thought his fellow Yale man, Dean Acheson, would knowingly or gladly tolerate them.

In this period, while Taft was underwriting violent attacks on Acheson, both were members of the Yale Corporation and their friends endlessly speculated as to what was said between these two when the Corporation met. The fact is that nothing was said between them—that is, nothing in a political way—so far as is recalled among their colleagues of the Corporation.

Though Acheson did not attend many meetings of the Corporation during the time when he was Secretary of State and Taft was suggesting over and over that the Secretary of

State was "soft" to communism, the Cabinet officer and the Senator *did* come together occasionally. Between them they appeared to have behaved with extraordinary correctness, avoiding all matters except matters pertaining to Yale and thus sparing their associates what inevitably would otherwise have been a remarkably sticky atmosphere.

There were men in the Yale Corporation who were appalled at Taft's attitude toward a fellow member; nevertheless, their affection for the Senator never varied nor did their tolerance of him basically decline. Acheson, for his part, plainly showed great forbearance; it cannot have been easy for him to deal at close quarters with Taft and keep the subject confined simply to the welfare of Yale. Nevertheless, this was what was done. "There was never the slightest political discussion between them," says the senior member of the Corporation, Bishop Henry Knox Sherrill.

Among Taft's complicated attitudes toward education was an attitude of friendliness to the concept, at least, of academic freedom that one can only suppose arose from or was strengthened by his associations with the other Yale governors. While neither in the period now under consideration nor later did he ever concede that any sort of Congressional investigation (under Republican sponsorship) had been unfair, he was nevertheless to observe in February of 1953, to the amazement of many old Taftites, that he would oppose the dismissal of a Communist teacher from a faculty unless that teacher was spreading Communist doctrine. This willingness to tolerate what might be called quiescent communism came, of course—and this is a point of the greatest relevancy—after Taft had lost his old sense of frustration.

To Taft, who took the view that the business of the opposition was "to oppose," partisanship was not only desirable but in a public man a public duty. And the rise of communism in the world frightened him to a degree that it had frightened few officials; he had thought it a greater menace to the world than fascism, even when fascism was overrunning Europe and before Stalin had started doing likewise.

More importantly, frustration's work had, at this point, turned his head. He reached the place where he was prepared to suspect, if not say, the very worst of almost any Democrat in power. He was able to assert flatly in early 1950 that the State Department with "its pro-Communist allies"—allies he did not name or otherwise identify—had deliberately turned China over to the Communists.

When General of the Army George C. Marshall was nominated by President Truman to be Secretary of Defense he came reluctantly forward out of an honorable retirement only because as an officer he regarded a Presidential wish as the equivalent of a command. He had been living, in vast weariness, in Leesburg, Virginia. He made it plain some months before to an interviewer that he felt that in all his years—as Army Chief of Staff, as Secretary of State, as sponsor for the Marshall Plan for Europe—he had now discharged his last proper duty and borne his last proper burden.

When, in these circumstances, the Marshall appointment

to be Secretary of Defense was before the Senate for confirmation in 1950, Senator William E. Jenner, Republican of Indiana, made a savage attack on the General, calling him, among other things, "a front man for traitors." Senator Leverett Saltonstall of Massachusetts could not stomach it and rose in horrified anger to General Marshall's defense.

Taft, as the responsible Republican head of the Senate, raised no voice at this. Indeed, asked by me in a Senate corridor whether his opposition to General Marshall was based in a dislike of having military men in civil posts, he replied with a chuckle: "Oh, I suppose that's as good a reason as any." The very best that could have been said of this episode on its face was that Taft was being unfair to all his traditions.

One who heard the remark cannot believe that the Senator really meant this dreadful apparent cynicism. His objection to Marshall probably was based primarily in the fact of the Marshall mission to China in 1945, which the orthodox Republicans have always claimed was a "sellout" of the Chinese Nationalists to the Communists. Nevertheless, there it was; this was Taft speaking.

These were not only unhappy days for his admirers but, in a sense, for Taft himself. A proud and self-contained man (sometimes a haughty one), he had no talent for acknowledging personal error and once he took a position, however untenable, his habit was to press on with it in a self-generating, rising bitterness. Nearly all that he permitted himself to stand for in these days alienated him from men who wished him well, some of them almost desperately so. Other powerful and well-placed conservatives felt, as sometimes had been said in another connection of Franklin Roosevelt, that Taft at minimum had let down his own class.

And this was the single area in his life about which one could not question him; he drew brusquely within himself on these points. He took any criticism, even from the most solidly conservative press, as calculated attack to promote the prospects of the Democrats.

The more his social and intellectual equals about the country fell away from him in this period the more it seemed that Taft, whose life motive had been before and again was to be *responsibility*, would go on until he had thrust them all away from him. It was said of him that he had become the greatest spendthrift of friendship in the Senate; this and other harsh and hard—and justified—things.

Where was the man who had been so big in the old Taft-Hartley days? Where was the old Taft awareness of the great obligations that go with great privilege? To what place had the old Taft gone? There were men who almost literally wept for Taft in those days, as men can weep when one who is both a great friend and a great man vanishes into the night. There had been a time when this man had been greatly underappreciated; now was a time when those who wished to believe the best had to face the hard fact of the worst.

Though come back home he did, and magnificently so, to become the old Taft again, this was the period that there began to be ranged against him the climactic forces that thereafter stood implacably between him and the White House, denying him what in so many ways he had so much right to aspire to. What was the meaning of these years? *Taft* knew how to lose the game; he did not know how to see the *Republican party* lose. And even in the years of his unlikely smallness—these worst years, and they were all of that—there was beneath it all something that was at least personally disinterested.

For during most of this time he was no longer thinking of the Presidency for himself; his concern was for the party. One could not escape the impression that in these years he allowed himself to think more of that party than of the Bill of Rights; here he ill-used his great inheritance.

☆ 8 ☆

RETURN FROM OHIO

Robert A. Taft's campaign for re-election to the Senate from Ohio in 1950 ended in a tremendous personal vindication for him, rather touchingly altered his own private view of himself and led him in 1951 to decide to try again for the Presidency. This had not been his intention in 1950; he told a friend, just at the beginning of his long, fierce struggle to return to the Senate, that he thought one more six-year term there would use up about all that was in him. And he added, with the strange, dry candor that was his, "I'll be pretty old by 1952."

He still suffered deeply at that time from the loss to which he considered Governor Dewey of New York had timidly and unnecessarily led the Republican Party as its 1948 Presidential nominee. His mood, as he viewed the prospects of his party nationally, was touched with a certain despondency. Moreover, though he often showed the bitterest of anger at the old slogan "Taft Can't Win," its constant repetition, if nothing else, had at least subconsciously had some effect on him. He was painfully aware, as he set out to plan his Ohio campaign, that he had absolutely no "glamour," a term and a personal characteristic he affected heartily to despise, but an attitude in which one believes there was more than a touch of wistfulness.

His authorship of the Taft-Hartley labor act and his eminence in the Senate—he was genuinely "Mr. Republican" there and where Taft sat sat the power—made the Ohio race from the beginning more a national than a state affair. The labor leaders (Taft called them "the labor bosses") were marshaling against him with such vast forces and in such panoplied array that one would have thought the White House itself to be the stake.

Taft's attitude at the start of this developing test was one rather of dogged determination than of high confidence, though this was all to change as the campaign progressed. One night in the spring of 1950 I entered a Washington restaurant to find Taft there dining alone. I joined him and during the meal half a dozen other diners, all of them strangers to him, came to the table to wish him well in Ohio. These little incidents, in which he showed an awkward pleasure in his reserved way, impressed him greatly. "You know," he said with a wry smile, "sometimes I think it a pity that voting is not restricted only to the fat cats. If that were only so, I could be elected to anything."

"Why all this, Senator?" he was asked.

"Look at those people who have come up to me," he said, "and look at what kind of a restaurant this is." The place, as it happened, was a reasonably expensive one; Taft, with his great literalness, could hardly imagine a New Deal *Democrat* entering there. More important to the present point, the anecdote illustrated what was then Taft's own understanding of Taft. He never gladly mixed with people in the mass; running for public office was tolerable to him only to the extent that he liked to discuss issues as much as he disliked the incessant handshaking, confusion and general disorder.

The way he campaigned in Ohio therefore qualified him not only as a stubborn man but as a brave one (it might be said that for at least part of the time he regained his proper stature) though to the average politician the task would perhaps not have been so very hard. There were hostile incidents—a thrown tomato, a wildcat strike in a plant occasioned by the fact that Taft had called there in his search for votes. It was not these, though, that challenged his courage; it was the endless fact that he had to meet so many thousands of people.

He went early at his work. He stumped all over Ohio in 1949 in what he called a "non-political report" to the people. In 1950, he went into every Ohio county. So proud was he of the Taft-Hartley Act that he ignored every counsel to soft-pedal that issue, or at all events not to go out looking for trouble on it. Everywhere and in every circumstance he invited, and even insisted upon, debate over the act.

By ordinary political standards he need not have done this so insistently; he could have contented himself by calling attention to the power that the State of Ohio had in Washington because of his place and prestige there.

While labor was taking all urgent steps to register labor voters and even to keep files on their individual status, Taft's people were going all the way to enlist business executives, professional men and women, farmers and every other sort of capitalist, small, middle and large. The thing took on some of the aspect of class warfare with Taft crying out against "a labor-socialist government" (that of Mr. Truman) and his Democratic opponent, Joseph Ferguson, and his associates presenting Taft as the picture of reaction and special privilege. They called him "a friend of the barons."

Taft, and quite characteristically so, identified himself not simply as one Republican running for re-election in Ohio but with the old Republican Eightieth Congress, which the voters had repudiated in 1948, and with the Republican party as a whole in its struggle to regain control.

"The general program of the Truman crusade," he said in a typical speech of that period, "is clear—promise everyone everything and hope to back it up with government money. Every American knows in his heart that such a policy will wreck the United States and reduce it to bankruptcy. It will bring first inflation and then depression."

Were the voters of the country, he asked, willing in 1950 "to turn over the country to Mr. Truman and a rubber stamp Congress," or would they elect a party (the Republicans) that "believes in liberty and Americanism and sound fiscal policy"? By the Democratic notion that freer world trade would promote all these things and peace as well, Taft was touched to the quick of his traditional, classical Republican partisanship. Such an argument, he declared, was only "a pipe dream."

Nevertheless, though he spoke with all his old harshness, he became to many a new man in a new face. The veteran political writer Gould Lincoln thus reported to the *Washing-*

ton Star from Portsmouth, Ohio: "Taft the statesman, Taft
the mine of facts, Taft the schoolmaster is an old story. But
Taft the man who can raise a laugh and can arouse an audi-
ence to personal and spontaneous enthusiasm is something
new. Yet, that's the Taft who is touring, day by day, the
eighty-six counties of Ohio."

While Taft concentrated in the campaign on domestic
matters, he turned many times to foreign policy. He accused
President Truman of having "usurped" the power of Congress in going to the rescue of the Republic of Korea when
the Communists invaded in June of 1950.

And he took time, in the middle of it all, to defend all
orthodox Republicans whenever and wherever and by whom-
ever they might be attacked. He denounced as only a reflection of "personal disappointment" a charge made by Hugh D.
Scott, Jr., of Pennsylvania, a former chairman of the Republican National Committee, that six Republican Old Guardists
in the South were not doing their best for their party because
they had been given "patronage and power" by local Democratic organizations.

"No one with any sense," Taft snapped, "would question
Carroll Reece's Republicanism." Reece, one of the six accused by Scott, was an old Taft man, as were the other five,
and was to participate heavily in Taft's last attempt at the
Presidential nomination in 1952.

In May of 1950 when two liberal Republicans—Senators
Wayne Morse in Oregon and James H. Duff in Pennsylvania
—won primary victories over the stout and futile resistance
of the old guard groups in their states, Taft declined to be

impressed. These, he said, were simply local matters and indicated nothing in the way of a rejection of traditional Republicanism.

Taft, as he did on many other occasions, attributed to the orthodox Republican party, and only that party, a proper resolution to deal with communism and a proper soundness toward spending money. "We need a Congress," he said, "which will not hesitate to pass the Mundt-Ferguson bill to require the registration of every Communist organization. We need a Congress which will investigate the vast government expenditures for the armed forces. What has happened to the vast sums of money already spent?"

He renewed a running fight with President Truman over economic controls, saying that the President was seeking "complete and arbitrary power" over the country's life. He rejected the argument that the Korean hostilities justified emergency controls. "I do not intend to say," he observed, "that the Korean war is not a real war or that it does not carry many of the heartbreaks and tragedies of a larger war. But, from the economic standpoint, it is not any particular strain on the economy of this country. Most of the materials needed are already in existence."

This somewhat airy treatment of what others thought was a quite obvious pressure on the economy rising from the war caused concern among some of Taft's own conservative backers in Ohio, who seemed always to be trying to persuade him not to be so prickly and not to go about violently hitting the exposed pocketbook nerve of the housewife. But he would not waver. No more candid a campaign could have been readily imagined.

As Taft had never conceded that controls would defeat inflation, he would not concede it now. Ohio associates learned what perhaps they had forgotten or never before known—that Taft, though an "Organization Man" all the way, was far more prepared to press his own views on any organization than to accept its views. Moreover, he was unwilling to appear to be even faintly a trimmer. Wherever and whenever his views were asked he gave them, with the flat, uncaring manner of a man hammering a nail into a board.

His friends and backers officially reported spending $243,000 in his re-election; he himself spent $1,529.14, as he meticulously reported, down, of course, to the last fourteen cents.

The bitterness of organized labor's attack upon him unquestionably helped rather than harmed him, for it was widely publicized that the powerful unions were sending in non-Ohio money and non-Ohio workers. Taft began to be presented as an Ohio victim of foreign forces, and this certainly did him no damage. Moreover, his opponent, State Auditor Joseph Ferguson, could hardly have been more suitable, from Taft's point of view. Ferguson, a spectacularly unlettered man, dropped grammatical bricks all over Ohio, so much so that his friends were driven to the argument that it was better to have in office a poor grammarian than a man who thought wrong on large issues.

Taft's fundamental integrity came greatly to his aid—and

so, oddly enough, did the powerful Democratic Governor of Ohio, Frank Lausche. Lausche dropped in the spring of 1950 a cryptic hint that *he*, the outstanding Democratic figure in Ohio, might well vote for Taft and not Ferguson. This extraordinary observation, which Lausche never amplified but never recanted, set the politicians all over the country to shaking their heads.

There were even suspicions that the national Democrats had somehow arranged, in the vulgar phrase, for the party to "go into the tank" for Taft in Ohio, that is, to see that he was not defeated in the notion of fattening him up for the slaughter if this success should lead the Republicans to give him the Presidential nomination in 1952.

There is no evidence to support this suggestion, which probably arose only from the undoubted fact that many of the Democratic professionals believed a Taft at the head of a national Republican ticket necessarily would mean the adoption by the Republicans of policies and attitudes that would lead to their defeat.

Ferguson, for his part, refused all the way through to debate with Taft—a wise decision but one on which the Taft people heavily capitalized because of its implied concession that the Democrat could not hold his own with the Senator in this field. The enigmatic Governor Lausche went on, meantime, taking actions that could hardly fail to be of aid and comfort to Taft. Both Lausche and the then Democratic mayor of Cleveland, Thomas Burke, gave to Ferguson the amazing snub of omitting even to formally endorse him at a meeting of the State Democratic party.

The Governor, for good measure, went on then to attack Ferguson's chief support, that of organized labor. Burke, incidentally, was appointed by Lausche in October of 1953 to be Taft's successor in the Senate.

In all these circumstances, Taft became what he had by no means been in the beginning—a certainty in Ohio. He beat Ferguson by 430,000 votes, one of the greatest margins ever given any candidate in Ohio.

He returned to Washington not only in elation, of course, but in an especially thoughtful frame of mind. It had been his real view before—and it was a correct one—that people generally did not storm the booths in their eagerness to vote for him. He had known, in short, that his personality was a difficult one. The Ohio result, however, set him to speculating earnestly about all this.

He was enormously proud of the obvious fact that people not remotely classifiable as "fat cats" had voted for him in great numbers, among them obviously many thousands of members of organized labor. He told me a few weeks after the election, with what was the closest approach to a tremor that I ever heard in his voice, that he had been astonished at what he considered to be this new friendship of "the laboring people."

He was at the same time not too keen about, or especially appreciative of, the backing that had been given to him by the business interests; he regarded all this simply as natural and his due.

The concept of a new relationship with labor moved him deeply, and the more so because whether or not the result was all that he had intended, it had never for a moment been his purpose in fashioning the Taft-Hartley Act to *hurt* laboring men. He had approached the whole question in the honest belief that the rank and file were in the grip of the "labor bosses."

He never to my knowledge said a word or took an action that indicated any contempt for or underappreciation of labor. Indeed, anything of the sort would have been quite alien to his hierarchy of values. Still, as unperceiving as he was so often in ordinary, common relationships, not even Taft had been able to close his eyes before and during the campaign to the storied hostility that organized labor, in its leadership at least, had felt for him and had developed against him.

When, therefore, his habitually careful and objective analysis of the Ohio election returns had shown him mathematically that laboring men as individuals plainly had wished him reasonably well, he had great joy. He felt that his explanations of the Taft-Hartley Act—which were never brilliant, because while he could strongly *insist* he never could really *explain*—had been thoroughly digested and rationally approved.

Independent inquiry in Ohio hardly indicates this to have been the case. There must have been many thousands in Ohio who voted for him in complete disapproval of his legislative record but in the instinctive feeling that there would be something historically incongruous in refusing to return to the Senate an Ohioan who was its most powerful member, a man of national and even world distinction. To understand

the position, moreover, it cannot too often be recalled that
the alternative, Joseph Ferguson, was so dim a figure that
even his fellow Democrats made it almost painfully plain
that they felt apologetic for him. And there was also the fact
that some labor men clearly resented being told so forcibly
how to vote.

Taft, for his part, never showed the slightest awareness of
these factors. He simply supposed that all the meaning of
the election returns could be read on their face: that Ohio
had very greatly preferred him, and *all that he represented*.
He made it clear to friends in Washington that he was now
prepared, upon due reflection, to discard the old image that
he had had of himself. The more he thought the thing over
the more he became convinced that he had miscalculated;
that he was a genuinely popular man and that it needed only
his type of campaign in Ohio, the smashing, rock-breaking
sort of campaign full of nothing but attack, to put him, or
any other really solid Republican, over anywhere.

The strongly operative qualification in this, however, was
the word "solid." It was not his view that just any kind of
Republican could win in 1952, even with a suitably Taft-like
campaign. It had to be the right sort of Republican; in plain
fact it had to be Taft, or someone very like him—and there
was no other very like him. This was Taft's logic at the time,
and there was nothing egotistical about it. He was simply
aware of the fact that without him his type of Republicanism
—and this was the only kind of Republicanism that was worth
having—had nowhere to go.

Accordingly, it had not been many weeks after the Ohio

election until he had planned in his own mind what was not to be announced for several months later—his third and last genuine thrust for the Presidential nomination. His sense of frustration with the national Republican party's prospects, which had led him into his period of irresponsibility, had not left him; but it was lightening.

Though it would be naïve beyond belief to take such a view of the protestations of politicians generally, many realistic men were and are convinced that Taft did in fact enter the lists in 1952 with a genuine if moderate sense of reluctance. He told some of his intimate friends that he was going to make the race because it seemed a logically indispensable action. Before him he had the specter of what he called "another Dewey." He felt that the Republican party simply could not survive unless it turned away from the Deweys and the Eastern internationalists in general. By this attitude he was, of course, writing off a very powerful—as it turned out, a decisively powerful—wing of the party. This did not trouble him in the least. He proceeded on the theory that millions of *his* kind of Republicans had not been voting for years in Presidential elections because they felt that the candidates were about as Tweedledee and Tweedledum. Accordingly, where other Republicans were setting out to find new ways of appealing to the independents and the young voters, Taft turned again to the past. His efforts were the reverse—not to convert the heathen but to bring the slothful backsliders back into the one fold.

His reckonings turned out to be inaccurate in two cardinal regards: The Ohio election had not in fact indicated that he had a special new popularity in the country, and again it was to be shown that in national conventions the East would continue to dominate the Republican party. Almost throughout its history, that party has managed to nominate for the Presidency men of more liberal view than the party's own composite views. If Taft was aware of this persistent tendency, he nevertheless thought it a wrong tendency and one that ought to be, and could be, reversed.

9

TAFT AND THE TWO GOP'S

For thirteen years, from 1940 to his death in 1953, Robert A. Taft and Thomas E. Dewey stood as the two great protagonists of the two Republican parties of the United States. The history of all this period of Republicanism was in the practical sense the history of these two men. Their titanic struggles with each other symbolized two whole ways of political thought and political life.

Taft represented, if not always exactly, a Republican party that was essentially old-fashioned, essentially isolationist, and had its hopes and policies based in the past. Dewey, with more exactness, represented a Republican party that was essentially forward-looking (Taft would have said spineless), dominantly internationalist, and willing as time went on to face one after another the realities of the political revolution that Woodrow Wilson had started and Franklin Roosevelt had carried to full power.

The Dewey Republican party, conditioned by the relative political sophistication of the East, began as early as 1940 to make accommodations with the Rooseveltian Democrats. What they could not lick the Dewey Republicans began to join, here and there, though maintaining a basic independence and remaining strongly partisan in their collective front.

The Taft Republicans, in plain truth, never came very close to grips at any time with the national Democratic organization, and never understood the degree and the sources of its power.

Though there were other and relatively minor factors—personal incompatibilities among them—these were the real factors in the long Taft-Dewey war. The Deweyites and the Taftites between them encompassed the whole Republican party, for in every real sense every Republican was one or the other; the party in all this period brought forward only these two schools of political thought.

The Taft Republicans took the position that nothing the Democrats had done, or might do, could be much good. The Dewey Republicans took the view that, both as a practical matter and as a matter of principle, it was necessary to assess the New Deal and then the Fair Deal in detail to select what ought to be maintained and what ought to be cast out. To Taft, in his political philosophy of either-or, this notion of the Deweyites was heretical. Worse, it was a kind of desertion in the face of the enemy.

The expression, "the Old Guard dies but it never surrenders," with all its implications of outmoded gallantry as well as its implications of simple obstinacy and majestic wrong-headedness, perfectly summed up the Taft Republicans.

Taft himself earned it to the end. In the last days of his life, as he lay in New York Hospital while a racing cancer ravaged him, he was told: "Governor Dewey wishes to see you."

"*Who?*" asked Taft incredulously. "Governor Dewey," was the reply. "I don't care to see *him* now," said Taft. "But," expostulated the attendant, "the Governor is already here; down in the lobby."

"Send him up, then," said Taft. Dewey had made the call in complete privacy; he had only come to say a good-by to a worthy foeman. What went on in that meeting this writer makes no pretense to know. Whatever it was, it must have been affecting, in this twilight time of a long divergence. These two had gone a long way apart and most of all they had parted because of the enormous difference in the view they took of the outer world and of the way in which the Republican party might best attempt to alter that world.

Dewey in his very early political days in New York had been touched with isolationism but by 1940 a great light had begun to fall upon him; the light of a world aflame. He had begun to see Britain's peril as distantly the peril of the United States and he had begun to feel, as it turned out that the majority in this country was feeling, that Britain must not fall. This was not, by present standards, by any means a clear-cut internationalist view, for at the time Dewey was speaking in generalities of "all proper aid" to "the victims of aggression." By those who recall the climate of 1940, however, it will be recalled that this was, for then, fairly strong stuff.

Taft, on the other hand, was approaching the crisis abroad with a characteristic sense of uneasy, troubled withdrawal. Deploring war almost with the intensity of a pacifist (his wife, Martha, was in fact a pacifist and always she had a vast influence upon him), his deepest conviction was only that nothing could be gained by any embroilment of the United States. When it came down to cases, what he really wanted to do was to stand apart.

In all these circumstances, there occurred at the Republican National Convention at Philadelphia in 1940 the first of the long series of Taft-Dewey confrontations by which the center of gravity of the Republican party was at length moved from the Midwest to somewhere near the Alleghenies. Here, at Philadelphia in 1940, began the slow but unbroken transfer of control from midlands to seaboard.

Never again, up to our present time, were the Taft kind of Republicans to be able to typify or control the national Republican party, though then, as now, they held a series of powerful local, regional and Congressional positions, like hedgehogs held in an otherwise unbroken military line.

And strangely, too, Philadelphia in 1940 saw what was to occur again in 1952—the emergence of an "outside man," not really identifiable as a past party in interest, who was to break Taft's ambitions. Wendell Willkie—like Dewey, a thoroughly transplanted Midwesterner—had been rising for some time in the public consciousness as an Eastern utilities corporation lawyer who was nevertheless able to take what was then a relatively composed view toward the incursions of Roosevelt's New Deal into the field of generating and selling electric power. Though he had fought the TVA he was able to do so calmly.

Willkie had been active in the moderately intellectual pursuits of the more liberal management groups of the Eastern

United States; he had, for example, been a valued speaker
before the Economic Club in New York. Dewey in 1940 was
only in local office, as District Attorney of New York County.
He had been defeated in 1938 in his attempt to succeed the
then Democratic Governor of New York, Herbert Lehman,
but only narrowly so and probably only because President
Franklin Roosevelt himself had gone to the aid of Lehman.

A vehement group of newly arrived politicians and internationalists took up Willkie as an alternative to Taft who was
acceptable to their design for a "modern" Republican party.
Two powerful Senators, Taft and the late Arthur H. Vandenberg of Michigan, therefore met at Philadelphia two other
Presidential contenders who were less well placed in the
official sense, Dewey and Willkie. Dewey and Willkie both
had, however, that most powerful of all qualities, fundamental acceptability to the East.

Though this may be hard to recall now, in light of the internationalist record he began to make after his "conversion"
at about the end of the Second World War, Vandenberg was
then far and away the leading isolationist of the lot. Taft,
though not out of sympathy with him in this field, was not
in so advanced a position; he was still primarily a domestic
man. Dewey, in the context of those times, could be described as slightly less interventionist than Willkie. The convention, by the way, had met in Philadelphia on June 24;
France had accepted the German armistice terms on the day
before, June 23. And President Roosevelt had just jolted the
Old Guard Republicans, whose leader, of course, was Taft,
by taking into his Cabinet two Republicans, Frank Knox to

be Secretary of the Navy and Henry L. Stimson to be Secretary of War.

This invitation, and most of all the fact that Knox and Stimson had accepted it, enraged the Taftites; they thought of it as a piecemeal surrender of a part of the Republican party that was never very reliable anyhow. Mr. Stimson was the very personification of the Eastern, interventionist Republican.

The newspaper files of the period will recall that, as usual, the Taft forces at Philadelphia were talking rather less than the others, and making fewer claims, but doing more acting, in a traditional way. Forty Republican members of Congress, representing more than two-thirds of the states that then had Republican members in the House of Representatives, issued a manifesto imploring the convention not to nominate such an atypical Republican as Willkie.

The balloting at Philadelphia took this course: Dewey on the first was far out ahead; he had 360 delegate votes to 129 for Taft, 105 for Willkie and 76 for Vandenberg. By the fifth and next to last ballot Dewey had sunk to 57 votes, Taft had reached his high point of 377 votes, Vandenberg was down to 42 votes and Willkie had thrust forward, commandingly, to 429 votes. He went on, on the sixth ballot, to win the nomination with 659 votes.

It was deeply significant that at this last, desperate juncture, when it was perfectly plain that by no rational forecast could Willkie be stopped, Taft still got 316 votes and Dewey declined to eight. All the way through, only Taft and Willkie had gathered strength at each new test in the balloting—

Willkie because it was thought he "could win," and Taft simply because he was Taft and because, as was true in two subsequent national conventions, he had the most faithful, unquestioning personal support of any candidate.

The 316 delegates who in 1940 stayed with Taft to the finish had done so under almost unbearable pressures. The bandwagon was careening off in the opposite direction. They were, each and all, taking a chance on a form of party ostracism, so strong is the notion that those who in these circumstances are not with a candidate are against him.

In the practical matter of bread-and-butter politics these Taftites were taking an open-eyed risk of being put upon a very thin political diet by the new Willkie Administration— if it came into being. Through it all, they stuck with Taft. In all but a few cases they probably were not aware of the historic nature of this contest, which was for the mind and spirit of the Republican party. They stood fast simply out of the hard loyalty that Taft both generated and himself practiced.

What had happened was both simple and complex. While it could be said that Dewey simply had not this time won, Taft had decisively lost; for the "Willkie Republicans" of this year were to become the "Dewey Republicans" of the future. Dewey himself in a sense had forecast and made possible the victory for Willkie, or more correctly the victory at the convention for a restrained approach, at least, to internationalism. For Dewey had defeated the arch-isolationist Vandenberg in the primaries in Wisconsin and Nebraska, which stood at the heart of the isolationist belt. And where Vandenberg had lost in these preliminaries Taft, too, had lost, and where Dewey had won in these preliminaries Willkie, too, in the same sense had won.

The ultimate power within the national party had come to rest in the East and the East had stamped its attitudes and complexion upon the national party. As for Taft, the generally seen, and less than fair, picture that had heretofore been somewhat vague of line now began to harden into clear focus. The picture was one of an obscurantist, a yesterday-man, and a loser.

For in spite of the fact that the convention's *platform* was full of rolling words of denunciation of "the excessive power" that the Democrats had vested in Franklin Roosevelt, and of warnings against foreign entanglements, these things came about: Willkie himself endorsed many New Deal reforms, really only maintaining that he could execute them better, and the now controlling part of the Republican party fell into step with the Democrats toward the ultimate intervention overseas.

To Taft's people, the Republicans had nominated in Willkie the first of what was to be, in the Taft view, a series of "me-too candidates." This had been accomplished, moreover, with the aid of public galleries that plainly had been packed, after the Taft people had been outmaneuvered in this regard, by pro-Willkie guests.

In the personal and literal sense of the word "control," Taft really controlled more delegates, out of their own choice, than any other aspirant at Philadelphia. But, as was twice again to be the case, when he had controlled these he had controlled all within his reach. Other, more flexible, more adaptable candidates were able in this convention and in others to start with fewer and finish with more, simply because while Taft's policies and attitudes were sometimes vulnerable to the slow erosion of an inward recognition of facts they were *never* alterable quickly or under any form of external pressure.

Taft himself liked to speak always of the "hard core" of his strength at convention time; the expression was more descriptive, perhaps, than he fully realized. It was as difficult for this hard core to expand as it was almost inconceivable for it to contract.

And not only was this the case. At the 1940 convention, and again in 1948 and in 1952, Taft's managers repeatedly suffered and caused him to suffer because of this rigidity. It was their desire and their habit to deal in absolutes; so many delegates equaling so much power in so many mathematical equations. It was their misfortune—and his—that their strengths were often their weaknesses.

Their limitless personal and ideological devotion to Taft was too fixed to permit them an adequate field of maneuver, even in Taft's own interest. Their meticulous and heavy-handed care in dealing with the obvious and palpable left them incapable of dealing well with the sudden and the intangible. They had, in the most literal sense, no subtlety at all; the merest office boy at any Taft headquarters showed this lack, equally with the highest manager.

Taft campaigns never lacked for money in quite adequate amounts but it was rarely money used with imagination. All was redolent of the old political techniques; one could very nearly smell the long-vanished fumes of the torchlight parades of Taft's own boyhood time. Of the money position in Philadelphia in 1940 Arthur Krock, the wisest and the best-connected political reporter on the scene, had this to say: "Taft's campaign has been lavish and organized to a degree not seen since Mark Hanna, also of Ohio, used to take care of such things for William McKinley."

All this—sufficient money, the indirectly applied power of the pro-Taft Congressional Republicans, the general weight of the Middle West, the more "professional" touch of the Taft managers, the infinitely greater political experience man for man of the Taft partisans—was not nearly enough. The Republican national convention of 1940, as the Taftites saw it, had committed a whole list of political errors. It had rejected Taft, it had adopted a platform that in no real sense squared with the attitudes shortly to be revealed by its Presidential nominee, and this nominee, if everything else was not bad enough, had in fact been a Democrat.

And while a historical process was set on foot that was to alter the whole face of the Republican party and the locus of its ultimate control—an achievement of the Deweyites and/or the then current Willkieites, who in this regard may be considered as one—a personal process set up its work in Taft.

This was to increase his suspicion of "the East," to make him for years later disinclined to consider Eastern Republicans as the genuine article, and in general to drive him back upon Middle West associations and attitudes not all of which in other circumstances would have been sympathetic to his view to the end.

10

CRISIS OF 1948

In the steamy early morning of June 20, 1948, Senator Robert A. Taft of Ohio set out from Washington accompanied by his wife, Martha, to drive in his small Plymouth car the 158 miles from Washington to Philadelphia, there to contend for the second time for the Republican Presidential nomination.

When he arrived in Philadelphia he had had two and a half hours sleep in the preceding seventy-two hours. He had stayed in Washington to the very close, at 4:00 A.M., of the Republican Eightieth Congress because as the real though then untitled Republican leader of the Senate he was unwilling to leave until the last word had been said. The Senate's final session alone had required forty-three hours of continuous sitting.

In Philadelphia he was met by Taft workers wearing little overseas caps and chanting a remarkable ditty that had been foisted upon the Senator by some eager submanager and which he had loyally adopted with a glazed uncomprehension that he tried his best to hide. "I'm Looking Over a Four Leaf Clover That I Overlooked Before"—thus sang the Taftites. The Senator, white with fatigue but attempting the unconvincing smile of a man who never could really smile except when he really wanted to, made his way at once to a hotel headquarters press conference.

Someone in the Taft organization, to give point to the fact that he was "Mr. Republican," had obtained and loosed in the room a live pygmy elephant, which careened about. Taft, who had been told so often by so many that he was not sufficiently "human," bore this like a gentleman. His manner was at once a pained resignation and an agreeable effort to be agreeable, if *this* was what people wanted.

His managers, having seen him lose before to other aspirants among whose attributes had been a superior sense of publicity, had set out this time upon the unlikely undertaking of making Taft folksy. He never pretended even faintly to understand such things; he assumed that the experts in such matters knew what they were about and so he let them have their way, though it was a rare experience to grasp his instinctive and suppressed response to these odd antics about him.

It was much as though an extremely sheltered elderly gentleman, determined to show all the good will on earth, had for the first time in his life come across a group of youngsters doing, let us say, the bunny-hop—but intending it to be in his honor. That is, Taft blinked owlishly; but, then, he supposed that there was this aspect, too, to politics. The synthetically "new" Taft, in short, had not himself been a conscious part of this process of modernization; but he was prepared to go along with it, much as he was prepared sometimes to go along with more questionable activities by political subordinates who had, as he thought, only his good at heart.

It was an odd thing, but the fact was that Taft, the traditionalist, had allowed himself to be surrounded by a kind of hucksterism whereas the "modern" Dewey, his great rival, was wrapped at Philadelphia in an invincible, remote dignity.

The difference, in its real meaning, could be expressed by a more meaningful illustration. The brisk and able Herbert Brownell, later the Attorney General in President Eisenhower's Cabinet, ran for Dewey as convention manager a campaign of smooth power, not especially seeking pictures in the newspapers but seeing to it that the Dewey visage was seen, when at all, in the best light. Representative Clarence Brown of Ohio, the Taft manager, was and is a small-town operator with many good qualities but with none of the perception of a Brownell in many matters.

Again there was illustrated here one of the fundamental distinctions between Taft and other politicians of his stature and power. He had the habit of selecting associates who, however worthy in themselves, were in no sense in his intellectual class. It was a characteristic—a failing or a blindness— that gravely troubled many Taft admirers, and some who were closer to him than mere admirers. It led some to have an anxiety for the future should Taft become President that was sharper than the anxiety arising even from such matters as his view of foreign policy.

In any event, at Philadelphia in 1948 this was the general scene: The Dewey people had in operation a machine of great expertness, mobility and acuteness. The Taft managers, as always, were characterized by the county-election, or at most the state-election, approach. Their experience, though great in terms of years, was somewhat remote and somewhat irrelevant.

It was said, in half jest but with something resembling the literal truth, that the Dewey organization could give a fairly accurate report on the whereabouts of a single one among the thousand-odd delegates at any hour of day or night. The Taft organization did not know where even most of the Taft people were, at any time. And the point is not so minor as perhaps it might look.

National political conventions are arenas of endless, wearing struggle and of sudden and passionate developments. Men can make mistakes, can be in the wrong place at the right time, for reasons far more forgivable than disloyalty or dereliction of duty. Communication and control from the candidate's central headquarters are absolutely vital. Even the momentary loss of this control and the momentary failure of this communication can be, in just the proper gathering of circumstances, cruelly damaging.

Such a failure occurred in 1948 at Philadelphia at the very outset of the convention at which Taft was again making his bid for the Presidential nomination. The first great issue there in a practical and immediate political way was which of the two competing Georgia delegations, the pro-Dewey slate or the pro-Taft slate, was to be accepted by the convention as duly chosen.

Sixteen delegate votes were involved; would they go in the showdown toward Taft's nomination or toward Dewey's nomination? The Republican National Committee, which had a pro-Dewey complexion, had decided, as the court of first jurisdiction, that the pro-Dewey delegation from Georgia should be seated. The Taft people had correctly anticipated this decision; their hope was in the convention's credentials committee, to which the issue now went on appeal.

Dewey's managers, having won in the national committee, offered to call off hostilities and to split the difference, giving eight Georgia delegates to Taft and eight to Dewey. This accommodation Taft indignantly refused. The Taftites by all ordinary reckoning could be expected to control the credentials committee, because of its general cast, but on the eve of the convention the great blow fell. The credentials committee, dividing 26 to 24, awarded all sixteen Georgia delegates to the Deweyites.

It seemed plain that the critical vote had been turned to the Dewey side by V. J. Washington, an Illinois member of the credentials committee and a Negro. It was a stalemated situation. Had he and one other gone, as had been generally expected, with Taft, then Dewey would have lost the decision. The Dewey position would, even in such a circumstance, have been less than desperate because the Dewey people could have appealed to the entire convention, where they looked a bit the stronger.

It is an entirely unrewarding business to attempt to attribute the responsibility for this critical loss to any single Taft manager or submanager; one can find almost as many accused scapegoats as there were Taft workers. Indeed, it may be that in the larger sense it was Taft himself who was to blame. As the Eightieth Congress drew to its noisy and bitterly controversial end, Taft was asked by reporters what action there would be on the civil rights program that so long had been promised both by the Republicans and Democrats.

Instead of offering polite evasions or pointing the accusing finger at somebody else—the Southern Democrats, for example, who were marshaled to filibuster any civil rights bill to the death—he characteristically took the responsibility, in the most untactful possible way. He simply replied, as was simply the truth, that civil rights "obviously" could not be acted upon in that session.

He gave no excuse for this and again, on arriving in Philadelphia, he returned to the question to observe tartly: "The Congress had forty pledges to perform on, and there is no reason to pick out that one [civil rights] more than any of the others." And he said it was up to the convention to back the record of that Republican Congress "on all points." What effect all this may have had upon the Negro delegates, the bulk of whom had always been considered historically Taft's, may only be conjectured.

At the very least, the outcome of the Georgia delegation fight set Taft on the road to his second great rejection by a Republican National Convention. His forces did not attempt to appeal beyond the credentials committee; having been unwisely bellicose in refusing an earlier compromise with the Deweyites they now were unduly timid in deciding not to make the try, at least, before the convention as a whole.

The loss was in a real, mathematical sense a considerable one and in the psychological sense it was incalculable. For it had for years been a recognized fact of political life that as he had controlled the majority of the Southern Republican Negroes Taft had controlled as well the generality of the Southern Republican organizations themselves.

The hard, alert Dewey people sprang upon the incident and powerfully exploited it; by nightfall of the first day of the convention it was being said "Taft Can't Win," this time that he could not win even a preliminary convention test on what had been his special home ground.

And then there came suddenly the hour of crisis for Taft. So well matched were he and Dewey in pledged or substantially pledged delegates that domination of the great, uncommitted delegation from Pennsylvania was the great indispensable of the convention. The untypical Eastern machine in Pennsylvania headed by Joe Grundy, long out of step with nearly all the rest of the Republican party in the East, was as old-fashioned as Taft himself. Grundy was out of power then in Pennsylvania in that the rebel James H. Duff was dominant in most of the state from the Governor's Mansion at Harrisburg. In any reasonably neat array of human affairs, Grundy would have *had* to be for Taft if Dewey was to be the alternative.

But, for a variety of reasons, it did not turn out that way. Grundy's people were said to have been promised heavy Republican patronage in Pennsylvania, where Duff was on the way to starving them out, if Dewey got the nomination, though Dewey implicitly denied this in a postnomination statement to the effect that he was without secret debt or commitment.

And old Mr. Grundy, for his part, was said, in a report that was far stronger than mere rumor but nevertheless a report that cannot be called a confirmed fact, to have been sadly horrified by Taft's un-Taftian stand for public housing and thus to have fallen into disenchantment.

Duff, an aggressively independent politician who later went to the Senate from Pennsylvania, was against Dewey but was, and is, a convinced and practicing internationalist and thus a typical Eastern Republican. He really wanted the Presidential nomination to go to Senator Arthur H. Vandenberg, who had now become the most useful internationalist in the Republican party, or perhaps to General Eisenhower. And it is fair, too, to say that Duff, one of the greatest fighters in political life, wanted to show old Mr. Grundy who was the new boss in Pennsylvania. Vandenberg persisted in keeping Duff and other would-be backers dangling to the end and Duff was thus at length thrown into the circumstance of having to back Taft simply because Vandenberg would not at that point "go," as they say in the political trade.

In this complex of affairs Duff and Grundy fell into a titanic battle for the control of the Pennsylvania delegation. When the debris had been carted out and air had been restored to a series of smoke-filled hotel rooms, Grundy was victor—in part. The armistice was this: Forty-one of Pennsylvania's votes would go to Dewey and twenty-seven to Taft.

This was really the end, though much anxious jockeying still went forward, for the Taft people could not now point to a single victory of substance in all their stand at Philadelphia. They went on trying desperately to stop Dewey. At one stage, Colonel Robert R. McCormick of the Chicago *Tribune,* an old Taft admirer from the Middle West, even suggested that Harold Stassen, internationalist and all, be taken aboard a Taft ticket—in second place, of course.

"I am glad," crowed Brownell, the Dewey manager, "that the Chicago *Tribune* ticket is out in the open at last."

Taft himself was then implored by some to come out for Vandenberg to force him to be a candidate, at least long enough to halt or deflect the rush to Dewey. This Taft refused to do. Vandenberg in fact had indicated to me before Philadelphia that he felt he had sacrificed his Presidential chances by his far-advanced internationalism but that the convention ought to choose an internationalist like Dewey. Vandenberg had said at the time that he would find the greatest pleasure in serving in a "foreign policy team" involving Dewey and John Foster Dulles, Dewey's adviser on foreign affairs.

Taft's view simply was that he had won the nomination as a matter of right, if only because he had mastered and operated the Eightieth Congress, the first all-Republican show since 1928, and because he alone of all nationally eminent Republicans had fought the Democrats every day and all the way. In the sense that anybody would have been more acceptable to him than Dewey, Taft might have gone in the last extremity, but for this feeling, to Vandenberg— though Vandenberg, in Taft's mind, had gravely compromised himself by his switch from long isolationism to internationalism. But not even this hard choice was open to Taft.

On the night of the opening of the convention's balloting, on June 24, he sat, far removed from all the noise and confusion, in a room at the Benjamin Franklin Hotel in Philadelphia. With him were Martha Taft and Jack Martin, his administrative assistant.

Taft picked up the telephone and one by one called his people momentarily away from their last exertions. He inquired meticulously and without excitement of the position in this or that critical delegation. The news was always the same: The Taft forces were characteristically resisting everywhere but they were being overborne. Without a word to Mrs. Taft or to Martin, Taft turned from the telephone, took up a long tablet of the yellow lawyer's notepaper that he liked to use, and began to write.

Out at the convention hall, Dewey on the first ballot had been given 434 votes to 224 for Taft. On the second, Taft moved up to 274—the Old Guard would not surrender here, either—but Dewey climbed to 515, or just 33 votes short of the 548 required to nominate. Before the third roll call could be started, Taft reached his Ohio colleague, Senator John W. Bricker, on the telephone, and Bricker then read to the convention the statement that Taft had drawn up in his hotel suite.

"A careful analysis of the situation," this said, "shows that the majority of the delegates will vote for the nomination of Governor Dewey. [By "vote for" Taft did not mean "favor."] I therefore release my delegates to vote for Governor Dewey, and to nominate him now." The convention then of course accepted Dewey by acclamation.

Taft the unchanging, Taft the man of the past, Taft who had refused all compromise (as in the Georgia incident)— again he had gone down to defeat. Though already the record of the Eightieth Congress was clearly raising a considerable public antipathy toward the Republicans, Taft had felt *responsible* for that Congress and he had gone to Philadelphia not merely accepting but even emphasizing this responsibility. In every way and at every turn he had spurned the easy way; always naturally resistant to making accommodations, he was literally unable in this case even to approach an accommodation, so profoundly did he believe that he personified the "right" and Dewey the "wrong" Republicans.

Though he bore himself well, the scars were many, and they never healed. And some things that were beyond Taft, but deeply involved him, now became clear. The conventions of 1940 and of 1944 (and it will be recalled that Taft was not active in 1944 in order to let Bricker seek the nomination) had been essentially repeated in 1948.

So powerful were the fundamental attitudes and policies of the Eastern Republicans, and so clearly were they now in control, that they had been able to nominate in Dewey a man who bore the stigma of having already lost to the Democrats, that is in 1944. And they had been able to reject in Taft a man who singly had dominated a Congress as perhaps no other in history had ever done. Taft felt that they had repudiated the record of the only enterprise that the

Republicans had been able even to put in motion in half a generation—the Eightieth Congress.

And this, in a way at least, they had certainly done; Dewey's subsequent campaign was by no means an apologia for that Congress, as it was by no means an all-out attack on Democratic persons or Democratic policies.

The dominant Republicans were still moving toward the future, whether or not their movement was wise. But the Taft Republicans still looked to the past, and the heavy weight of their accumulated failures to control or even really to impress their wishes on the national party rested heaviest of all upon his own bald, strong head. For he *was* the Taft Republicans; intellectually and in point of necessary prestige he was all that they had. And for support they were, in any hour of last decision, all that *he* had.

III.

TAFT AND FOREIGN POLICY

☆ 11 ☆

THE LAST SPEECH

The last major speech made by Senator Robert A. Taft was on foreign policy, a subject that of all possible subjects was the least appealing to him. It was made by a gravely sick man who knew that he was in all probability also a dying man. It was made not so much for posterity as to please an old friend, at the incidental expense of deeply troubling the Republican Administration of President Eisenhower, to which at this time Taft was on the whole giving a last, full service of help and loyalty.

It shocked the Allied world, for at this time the United Nations was feverishly and in an atmosphere of the greatest delicacy in search of a truce in Korea. It was all done by the Republican leader of the United States Senate, a man whose power and responsibility was then almost co-equal to that of the President himself, as a favor to Mr. Benjamin Katz of Cincinnati, Ohio. If Taft ever saw any incongruity in it all, he never indicated that he did.

Benjamin Katz of Cincinnati was the local head of the National Conference of Christians and Jews. He was a Taft man from the distant past. There had also been a long personal association and, indeed, even a client-attorney rela-

tion, for Taft's old law firm in Cincinnati had long represented the watch company that Katz headed.

Several times Katz, as a Zionist, a position toward which
Taft himself had the greatest sympathy, had asked the Senator to take part in the affairs of the Conference and always,
for one urgent reason or another, Taft had been unable to
do so. But on this occasion, he was more or less immobilized.
He was a patient in the Holmes Memorial Hospital in Cincinnati—he was there because he had cancer—and he felt
that now he could oblige Katz, to whom he was greatly
devoted.

Thus, on May 26, 1953, Taft wrote out a speech—in which,
among other things, there was a declaration that the United
States "might as well forget the United Nations so far as the
Korean war is concerned"—that he proposed to deliver by
telephone from the hospital to the Conference in its meeting
in the Netherland Plaza Hotel in Cincinnati. It turned out
not to be feasible to do this by telephone, but Taft, whose
own private thoughts and private sufferings were kept strictly
private, did not let this deter him.

He handed the manuscript over to Robert A. Taft, Jr., and
Young Bob stolidly went to the hotel and read it. After recalling his old support of the concept of an independent
Israel, the Senator's paper went forward to the main business at hand, which was to suggest that if the current negotiations in Korea failed then we should simply take "a free
hand" in Asia.

It was in some ways a characteristic, though by no means
an exactly typical, Taft foreign-policy address, for reasons

that will be pointed out a little later. Its one dominant theme was the expression of a kind of philosophic helplessness.

The whole present policy of resisting communism, said Taft, was not really a policy of working through the United Nations—even though the entire Republican Administration was, of course, totally committed to the United Nations as the greatest stone upon which to rest its position in world affairs. What we really were doing, Taft went on, was operating under the shelter of a military alliance.

"It is an attempt to build up freedom throughout the world and provide arms for all those nations which are sufficiently free so we can be reasonably certain or reasonably hopeful that they will use their arms to fight the Communists if they are attacked.

"The difficulty with the United Nations as a means of preventing military aggression was obvious from the beginning. I pointed out in the first speech I made in favor of ratifying the United Nations treaty (Charter) that it could not possibly prevent aggression because of the veto power which could be used by any one of the five (great) Powers to veto united action against themselves and against any of their satellites.

"The United Nations was based on the theory of a five-Power control of the world, and whenever one of these Powers refused to go along it was hopeless to create any sanctions that would be binding on the other nations to provide troops against aggression. We made an abortive attempt to rely on the United Nations when the North Koreans attacked in 1950. It happened that the Russians were boy-cotting the Security Council, and so we were able to persuade the others to call for troops from all members against the North Koreans.

"There is some doubt whether the call was a valid call even then, because the Charter clearly requires the affirmative vote of all of the five controlling nations, and I don't think that absence provides an affirmative vote.

"Nevertheless, it was treated as a proper sanction and produced a few troops, in addition to those which we had sent to Korea. But Russia refused to return to the Security Council and when Communist China attacked then the United Nations failed to take any action against the real aggressor, and from that time until today has refused in every way to take action or punish the real aggressor.

"There has been some attempt to substitute the General Assembly as a body which can call on nations to join in defeating an aggressor, but the General Assembly has absolutely no such power under the United Nations Charter. It is very doubtful to me whether we would be wise to try to set up and develop any such power. In an assembly where we have one vote out of seventy, it can be easily turned against us in the future.

"I believe we might as well forget the United Nations as far as the Korean war is concerned. I think we should do our best now to negotiate this truce and if we fail then let England and our other Allies know that we are withdrawing from all further peace negotiations in Korea.

"Even the best truce under present conditions will be extremely unsatisfactory. It will divide Korea along an unnatural line and create an unstable condition likely to bring war again at any moment. It will release a million Chinese soldiers, who no doubt will promptly be moved down to Southern China for use against Chiang Kai-shek or against the French in Indo-China.

"It seems to me that from the beginning we should have insisted on a general peace negotiation with China, including a unification of Korea under free Koreans, and a pledge against further expansion in Southeast Asia. If we once make this present truce, no matter what we put in the agreement about further negotiations for a united Korea it is no more likely to occur than a united Germany.

"In any event, I think we are bound to the policy of preventing Communist aggression where it occurs and where it is in our power to stop it. I have never felt that we should send American soldiers to the Continent of Asia, which, of course, includes China proper and Indo-China, simply because we are so outnumbered in fighting a land war on the Continent of Asia that it would bring about complete exhaustion even if we were able to win.

"I believe we might as well abandon any idea of working with the United Nations in the East and reserve to ourselves a completely free hand.

"This statement is going to shock a good many people who still believe in the United Nations. I believe in the United Nations myself but not as an effective means to prevent aggression. It does have many methods by which, through peaceful persuasion, it can defer and prevent war.

". . . But no one should be shocked at my suggestion about the United Nations in Korea, because in Europe we have practically abandoned it entirely. When we adopted the North Atlantic Treaty we did not ask the United Nations' leave, and we did not consult it. We claim that such an organization can be formed under the terms of Section 51 of the Charter and perhaps it can. But in my mind it is the complete antithesis of the Charter itself and while it may not violate the Charter it certainly substitutes a military alliance for the United Nations as a means of preventing Soviet aggression.

"NATO, following the Greek and Turkish agreements and the contemplated arrangements with Spain, is clearly a military alliance of the old type. We promised to spring to the aid of any nation which is attacked, either by the Russians or by any other nation, including one of the NATO group. Our obligation continues for twenty years.

"So today, as since 1947 in Europe and 1950 in Asia, we are really trying to arm the world against Communist Russia, or at least furnish all the assistance which can be of use to them in opposing Communism. Is this policy of uniting the free world against Communism in time of peace going to be a practical long-term policy? I have always been a skeptic on the subject of the military practicability of NATO. I am no military expert but I have never heard an argument that impressed me attempting to show that United States ground forces could effectively defend Europe.

"Certainly we seem to have undertaken to defend countries like Norway and Denmark, which it would be almost impossible to defend in case of a sudden Russian attack.

"I have always felt that we should not attempt to fight Russia on the ground on the Continent of Europe any more than we should attempt to fight China on the Continent of Asia. I have always felt that that defense must be undertaken by those who occupy Western Europe. After all, there are at least 225,000,000 of them, fifty per cent more people than we have in the United States.

"I have always been concerned that once our troops are in Europe, the Russians would be able to bomb all the factories and communications lines behind them. One atomic bomb would probably destroy a French port for a year, and eight or ten bombs would cut off most means of supplying our soldiers or withdrawing them in case of retreat.

"If we are worried here in this country about the dropping of Russian bombs on American cities and factories, surely it is ten times as easy for them to bomb Western Europe and its ports.

"Or they could leave Europe alone and devote themselves to bombing this country, in which case our European expenses would be of doubtful value.

"But there is another difficulty about maintaining the general policy of a unified world-wide opposition to Communism by all free nations: We have to have not only the written word but the real sympathetic support of our Allies in that job. Recent events in France and England indicate that they are more than anxious to settle with Russia and resume as much trade as possible, which means that as long as Russia talks nicely the whole military alliance is weak, even though military preparations behind the lines continue unabated.

"Secretary Dulles has tried to reassure the Iron Curtain nations that we are not going to make a deal with Russia giving the Communists a zone of influence over all the Iron Curtain countries. It seems clear that Mr. Churchill and the French administration would be willing to assign that zone of influence gladly and abandon the Poles, the Czechs, the Hungarians and the Rumanians to the tender mercies of Soviet Russia in return for some cut in armaments, freer trade and promises to behave in the future.

"The present Administration has the job of trying to maintain the world-wide alliance against Soviet Russia. We have spent billions for that purpose. I hope that it can be carried through and only raise here the doubt as to whether it is in fact possible over any long period of years."

So, with all this, which so far as it went was the authentically despondent voice of Taft on foreign policy, what remained in the way of hope? The United Nations? Certainly not. For Taft, though he had voted for it, had known all along that it would not amount to very much.

The "military alliance" that in his view had supplanted and usurped the United Nations? Certainly not. For we probably could not long sustain it; and anyway it was clear that while this was a military alliance none of the Allies within it could well be trusted. To arm Europe alone? Hardly: for one could have no assurance at all that Europe would fight.

To retire from it all? Yes; this was the answer, though it was not stated as such.

The response to all this among nearly all shades of internationalism was violent, and justifiably so. An outcry arose that Taft was proposing that we "go it alone." He never used that expression, and to this extent the characterization was inaccurate. The *meaning* of his speech, however, was precisely this and no other, for if one had to have "a free hand" in Asia and could trust none of his ostensible Allies in Europe where in the world could he be other than "alone"?

The *New York Times,* saying in substance what many other persons and publications were saying, declared editorially: "Senator Taft is a confusing man. Moreover, he is not always as consistent as he might be, and his sense of timing now and then lacks the touch of the true statesman. The Senator's remarkable speech . . . is what again gives rise to such judgments on his ideas.

"The confusion is a basic one, for when the speech is analyzed one sees that it is essentially a defense of isolationism in a world where isolationism is impossible.

"Mr. Taft apparently wishes us to withdraw our troops from the European Continent, since they might be cut off by Russian bombing of 'all the factories and communications lines' behind our forces. Setting aside the fact that the Senator's calmness in contemplating the annihilation of Western Europe has more than once distressed our European Allies, there is another confusion involved. The Senator in his speech condemned Britain and France for a supposed willingness to 'abandon the Poles, the Czechs, the Hungarians and the Rumanians to the tender mercies of Soviet Russia.' Yet what is he planning to do with his withdrawal of troops? Americans cannot at one and the same time be isolationists and liberators. . . .

"How are we to gain Mr. Taft's objectives in China and Korea if we 'withdrew'?"

The White House for a day remained in embarrassed silence and then, on May 28, President Eisenhower disavowed Taft, though in the most gentle, kindly way. Taft, the President said, was certainly entitled to his own opinion; nevertheless the President did not agree with that opinion.

Taft himself, returning to Washington from the hospital in Cincinnati, as always rode out the storm. He never backed up on a word, though he did point out that he had never used the phrase "Go it alone."

What was remarkable about this last Cincinnati speech—the last studied utterance of consequence by Taft on any subject—was not that he had so far upset things but that it had all been, for him, so mild. He now said, for example, this man who in the years before had so insistently accused the Truman Administration of an out-and-out hospitality to communism, that the Truman Administration "certainly believed in the general policy of opposition to Communism."

He observed at Cincinnati, too, that from his seat in the Foreign Relations Committee he had become "impressed with the tremendous difficulty of all of them [foreign problems] and the fact that in no case does there seem to be a satisfactory solution." It may be that this was of some slight, delayed comfort to Dean Acheson, to George Marshall, and to all those others upon whom for years Taft had poured a fire of unrestrained denunciation.

And, finally, like a man suddenly bereft of a dozen old positive certainties, he had concluded at Cincinnati: "All that I can urge is two different kinds of tolerance to this tolerant body. The first is that we be tolerant of the situation in every country, that we try to understand their problems and not force upon them a policy they do not approve, either by the pressure of grants of money or grants of soldiers. No doubt they will be glad to get these but they will be of little use to us unless the policy they are supposed to enforce is the determined policy of the country concerned.

"Second, I urge upon you tolerance of those who are trying their best to conduct our foreign affairs. I think already they know more about the realities of the situation than those who preceded them. I know that they are inspired with the best of good will toward all nations. They have to meet what seems to me the most difficult problems of foreign policy the United States has ever faced."

Nowhere had he pointed to a single place in which in any major way President Eisenhower and Dulles had altered the policies that in the hands of Mr. Truman and Acheson had been so disgraceful. Indeed, these continuing policies offered nothing but the thinnest of hope, at the very best.

What was one to make of all this? Here was a Taft acknowledging that Truman and Acheson really had at least *wanted* to oppose communism; a Taft acknowledging that nothing about any of it was indisputable or easy; a Taft urging a *tolerant* view, even toward those with whom one might fundamentally disagree.

This was, in the field of foreign policy, the last inconsistency of a hundred inconsistencies, though this time a genial one, of a man whose record in world affairs was inconsistent almost to the point of inconceivability.

12

ON WAR AND PEACE

T aft not only failed all his life to develop a coherent view of a proper foreign policy for the United States— he was endlessly contradicting himself—but he felt alien to and fearful of the whole world scene. He was, in dealing with such matters, like an Admiral who strongly dislikes the sea.

The practical *effect* of nearly all his actions in this field as a powerful United States Senator was to promote isolationism. The *motives* of his actions were in some cases, though not in all, actually not isolationist. The circumstance that he was not an America Firster outright and always can only be explained by the fact that while he had some of the Midwestern attitude of resistance to foreign ideas and events simply because they were foreign, this attitude did not in his case spring alone from mere chauvinism or a lack of objective generosity.

And while he often symbolized Midwestern isolationism he never spoke wholly for that view of the world and that view never wholly dominated him. The Midwest view, which since 1914 had been expressed in desperate and losing struggles to keep us in a state of apartness from Europe in two world wars with the Germans, plainly was based in part on ethnic considerations—or in blunter words on the fact that many people of German descent and fond German memories lived in the Midwest.

There was no sentimental sighing for the glories of Old Heidelberg and so on in Taft's reasoning. And in perhaps the most famous of his isolationist actions—his vote against Senate ratification of the North Atlantic Treaty alliance— his position in some senses was very strong. (It was incidentally, and quite unintentionally, a great relief to the Europeans, who wanted the treaty to mean what it said.)

In a famous Senate debate with John Foster Dulles, then a Senator from New York and later President Eisenhower's Secretary of State, Taft's very attacks on the treaty helped clothe it in dignity and meaning simply because he insisted on pointing out that it *did* commit us to plain and naked force—if that became necessary to save the free West. Dulles and to some degree most of his pro-treaty associates dealt primarily in worthy generalities and tended to be rather gingerly when it came to talking of the obligations involved.

At the high point of a long Senate passage at arms in 1949 this, for example, was the position:

Taft (ironically): ". . . The Senator's [Dulles'] conclusion is that the ratification of the pact imposes no legal or moral obligations to aid any one of the eleven nations who have signed the pact, that is, by providing arms? Is that a correct statement of the Senator's conclusions?"

Dulles: "I said in substance that I see in the treaty no legal or moral obligation to vote any arms program which is not defensible on its merits." There was nothing, in this

reply, that seemed quite to fit the overmastering characteristic of the alliance—its clear, unqualified pledge of all for
one and one for all.

In a legal sense, Taft actually had an internationalist view
—that is, order and justice, if they could be tidily achieved,
were to him as important to Iceland and as justifiably sought
there as to Ohio.

He was always, of course, a bookish, intensely studious
man and he was not impervious to facts, provided that he
could search these out for himself (or, if it came to the
worst, obtain them from persons in whom he had unshakable
confidence). In the area of world affairs, as in many others,
the *sources* of information were to him almost as important,
in determining whether his mood would be one of acceptance
or rejection, as was the information itself.

It so happened that for far the greater part of his public
life he had no opportunity, or no compelling need, to get at
the facts of the world lying outside the United States. He
was, but for the last two or three years of his career, a
strictly domestic political leader. He gloried in that and
privately he took the view that most Senators whose eminence
lay in foreign policy were a posturing and faintly ridiculous
lot of men. He watched with an inner derision the movement
away from isolationism that was led from early 1945 onward
by Senator Arthur H. Vandenberg of Michigan, who had
been in his time the outstanding, all-out isolationist of the
Senate.

Skeptical of converts in any phase of life, Taft, while not
challenging Vandenberg's sincerity, really thought that his

old colleague had gone a little soft in the head—probably
from the blandishments of "the internationalists," to whom
Taft always attributed a flatteringly excessive and fatal
charm upon all but the most rugged political characters.

In the years of the so-called divided Senate Republican
leadership—that is, Taft on national matters and Vandenberg
on international matters—"Mr. Republican" had the greatest
misgivings in letting Vandenberg have his head. He only
found it possible to do so because "Van" was, after all, a
Republican, though by now a very doubtful kind of Republican.

And as Vandenberg went forward with the concept of
bipartisanship in foreign policy, it was only by iron self-
restraint that Taft was able to avoid making mocking noises
in public. Apart from the fact that he simply was one of the
most intensely partisan men in the recent history of American politics, he had great philosophic veneration of the
two-party system. He deeply believed that it was this system
that made the parliamentary life—and free enterprise—possible. Thus to him any softening in the harsh, natural,
ordained friction between leadership and opposition could
be mortally dangerous to the whole health of the American
political system.

His narrow, highly traditional view of bipartisanship was
that it was ninety per cent cant and nonsense, and this was
in fact a view that was privately shared in some degree by
nearly every man in the Senate who was a genuinely typical
"Senate man," meaning an institutionalist to whom the
Senate and its inner procedures came first before the world

outside. And the Taft opinion of the bipartisans was helped along by the undoubted fact that in the strictest sense there *was* something illogical in that tremendously sound concept, as there is in many of the concepts of government with which Britain has endowed the English-speaking world.

Many a bipartisan of the postwar world had read the election returns, though he had no doubt read other things, too, and to Taft this fact alone made them a suspect breed. To him the election returns were rarely as they should have been—and in any case not necessarily controlling, and never, as he saw it, a justification for what he considered to be political trimming.

His attitude toward Vandenberg, therefore, was a difficult one. So strong was his sense of the proprieties, and his sense of proprietorship in the Republican party, that I never heard him criticize Vandenberg in private, though infrequently he was irresistibly moved to do so in public.

Vandenberg, a wise and tolerant man who nevertheless lacked both the essential influence in the Senate and the raw courage that Taft had, moved with great care and discretion during the period of his bipartisan leadership. He knew that fundamentally he could convince Taft at best of very few things and so when it fell out that he had a foreign bill to manage in the Senate he would go not to Taft but to a Taft friend and suitable intellectual associate, Senator Eugene D. Millikin of Colorado.

Millikin—who, it goes without saying, was an old Taft man politically—would act as go-between and intercessor. He could thus accomplish what Vandenberg never could have.

He could, usually, bring about a reluctant and uneasy and temporary Taft silence so that Vandenberg could have a breathing space.

It was therefore not until 1951 that Taft began to take a direct and personal as distinguished from a remote, faintly hostile interest in foreign policy. Vandenberg tragically died in April of that year. And, apart from the fact that his overwhelming re-election to the Senate from Ohio in November of 1950 had led him to decide to try again for the Presidency, Taft felt compelled to make the attempt at becoming a foreign policy expert.

Shortly after returning victorious from Ohio, and at a time when Vandenberg already was all but out of the running because of his illness, Taft told me with great gusto of his many plans in the field of domestic legislation. "What about foreign policy?" he was asked. A shadow fell over his face and he replied: "I wish I could just stay out of that; but of course I can't." Later, he said publicly: "I am charged with moving in on foreign policy; the truth is that foreign policy has moved in on me."

He knew then—indeed he almost conceded it—that his tremendous exertions on domestic bills and the demands made by his general Republican leadership in the Senate had left him no time or forum in which to understand world affairs and that he was entering here as a novice.

It is entirely possible, and even probable, that in other circumstances the novitiate might have been a successful one; but again the fact that he was Taft stood as an unbreakable barrier to this. It was literally not possible for him to deal in any policy matter on any sort of easy, conversational terms with any Democratic bureaucratic officeholder, in the State Department or out of it. Thus, the very men who had the requisite information of the world never crossed his path. Those who "briefed" him, even if their views had been right, were not in responsible positions. The State Department people, for their part, would never have dreamed of accosting Taft with their data; he would not have thought of calling on them.

The personal qualities that in this regard stood in the way of his education stood in the way elsewhere as well. As has been suggested earlier, to understand anything it was necessary to him to know it in a *personal* sense. He knew in the personal sense little of the operations of diplomacy and almost nothing, because of the circumstances of his life, of the infinitely complicated and interrelated matter of military policy and practice.

He not only abhorred war, as was of course entirely to his credit, but had a conception of it that can only be described as most remote. It was his habit, for example, to refer to a Commanding General as "the man in charge." He had an immovably mercantile view toward military expenditures and tended to believe that these could be safely altered much as a merchant would alter his invoices in a poor season, on wholly economic grounds.

It was because of this opinion that he seemed endlessly to be putting price tags on military security, in this nation or among its Allies; seemed endlessly to be attempting to cut foreign aid by some fixed, arbitrary percentage point. He

really saw the conduct of military policy as not much different, at the top, from the conduct of a banking enterprise.
The highest possible priority was solvency, in spite of the
fact that the solvency of a military establishment is not meas-
ured in the same way as the solvency of a bonding house.

War's dirtiness and horror and above all general wasteful-
ness properly appalled him. But that a point could be
reached in which a just war was morally inevitable, dirt and
all—this he could hardly grasp. This was why he could say,
as he did in 1940 when Britain was alone (and as he repeated
to me in 1951) that for the United States to enter the war
in aid of Britain would be "even worse than a German victory."

It ought to be understood that he was not consciously
heartless in this but only that he had a view that the only
indispensable thing was to protect "American liberty," which
he believed to be quite divisible from liberty in general. He
had the conviction that war, almost any war for almost any
purpose, would only end in a totalitarian world. He felt this
not so much for ideological reasons, but, as he once said in
1939, simply because it might pragmatically force "the
nationalization of all industry and all capital and all labor"
and thus "create a Socialist dictatorship."

In 1940 he declared in Congress: "It is said that our foreign
trade would be destroyed [meaning if Britain went down].
I don't understand why, if peace is once restored, we could
not trade as well with Germany as with England."

All through the decisive period of the last of the thirties
and the opening of the forties he stood against any form of

American intervention. He opposed the draft before Pearl
Harbor. He opposed arming the American merchant ships.
He opposed the repeal of the Neutrality Act. He opposed
lend-lease.

In 1951, in his book *A Foreign Policy for Americans,* he
declared that his view had been that "we should aid Britain
as much as possible, consistent with staying out of the war."
The trouble was that in the days of crisis it had seemed that
the qualification "as much as possible" was altogether controlling. Almost nothing seemed in those days to Taft to be
possible.

And in the same book he recalled that he had voted against
the draft in 1940. But now he said: "I have always been in
favor of a conscription bill in time of war or in case war is
threatened and voluntary methods failed." Before this, he
had said simply that the draft was "totalitarian" and therefore supremely unacceptable.

In the war years and later he ridiculed any theory that
Nazi Germany had ever raised any danger to the United
States. He said to me as late as November of 1951 that at no
time had Germany menaced the security of the United
States and that there would have been no menace even had
the British fallen, "and particularly not after the Russians
had entered the war against the Germans."

Through it all, until we ourselves went in, he refused to
see any real and overriding moral issue as involved in the
war. He said in Congress in 1943: "What difference does it
make if Franco is a Fascist or a Communist so long as the
net result . . . is a direct aid to our military effort? Italy

and its opera bouffe Mussolini have never been a real menace."

In 1944 he declared in Congress: "The ultimate purpose of our foreign policy is not to bring peace into the world, but to secure *our own* [italics mine] freedom by preventing the rise of an aggressor who will cause another world war into which we may be drawn. World peace is a means to that end. We are interested in world peace because world war threatens our own security."

But again, in his book in 1951 he said: "If we confine our activities to the field of moral leadership we shall be successful if our philosophy is sound *and appeals to the people of the world.*" (Italics mine.)

These quotations are reproduced in part to show that something had happened to Taft's thinking between 1944, when in a single sentence he seemed to dismiss the idea of bringing "peace into the world," and in 1951 when he suggested that our moral position must be one that would appeal "to the people of the world." His own first position, whatever else might be said of it, can hardly have had that appeal. Primarily, however, the effort here at the moment is to attempt to suggest the complexity and the elusiveness of Taft's general philosophy on peace and war.

This general view is not easy to describe. It was, I think, founded most of all on Taft's deep conviction that the most meaningful thing in the world was the liberty of the individual American—a liberty based on the three requirements of a free enterprise system, national independence and political democracy. He recognized that war *could* destroy all three and because this was so he refused always to look at the other side of the medal. That failing to enter a war for survival, or refusing to aid others who were fighting the common peril, could destroy all these three—and much more.

And his own view was not simply that war was too desperate an expedient, considering that one could always lose it. He thought, too, that preparations for war could themselves defeat liberty, because they would or might involve the imposition of Federal controls on the economy. In the end, his position really was that we must be careful not only to stay out of war but to avoid the only posture of defense that was likely to keep us out of war. For, in his view, sufficient preparation was likely to be almost as bad as war itself.

It was in part this conviction that led him late in life to become one of the foremost, and extreme, advocates of a military readiness based almost wholly upon the sea and air arms. These, at least before the full onset of the new and emerging atomic weapons, were vastly cheaper to maintain than the dozens or scores or hundreds of infantry divisions that might be required.

But this cost element was not the sole reason. The human reason back of all this was Taft's strong sense of paternalism. It was to him a terrible thing to vote to put a boy on a muddy field of fire and the more so, I believe, because he was aware that by the accidents of his own life he himself had never been confronted with such a sacrifice. He was a small man here and there and now and again. But in the whole slope of his life and purposes he was a large man, and it was a great bitterness in him to seek to require of another what he had not done or could not do himself.

He told me in 1951, in the period when he was first clamoring for a reassessment of foreign-military policy to give practically all the emphasis to sea-air, that his proposal had been influenced, if not shaped, by "certain reading" he had been doing. "What reading, Senator?" he was asked. "I have gone very carefully again over the history of the Napoleonic campaigns," he replied. "Wellington at Waterloo accomplished what he did with only twenty per cent of his troops from the United Kingdom and the rest mercenaries."

He had, in short, by a strange paradox, a compulsive bias toward the most traditionally professional of all professional military opinion. He believed that what Britain had done in the eighteenth century by her control of the sea the United States and Britain, with Britain of course the lesser partner, could do past the halfway mark in the twentieth century.

In this regard he saw air power as only an extension of the sea arm. And because of his hesitations, because of his lively but uncomprehending compassion for the nasty job of the infantry, he gladly accepted one of the special prejudices of the old-fashioned Admirals—their prejudice against a war of mass and especially against having to use vast numbers of amateurs in the shape of quickly impressed civilians. Taft could readily understand this; *he* did not like amateurs in political campaigns.

In sum, the traditional view suited him exactly. It was relatively cheap. It would involve mainly men trained in and prepared to accept the hazards of war as a way of life. It would, as he saw it, upset the domestic economy to the least possible extent and cause the fewest possible controls. And it would at all events turn over to people to whom it would mean the least self-sacrifice the most helter-skelter and doubtful business of warmaking.

If one understands this, he can then understand at least, though he need not accept the explanation as a valid one, why Taft was so ready to predict that great horrors would fall upon continental Europe. When he accepted his thesis that war could be prevented—or at worst, won—by the West through sea-air power, even though the antagonist, Russia, would be the largest land-infantry power in history, the continental mass in Europe became logically expendable.

The British Isles, on the other hand, *became* indispensable, and this priority—though he did so much so often to offend the British people—those islands held in much of his postwar thinking. For the British Isles were, of course, to form the left sea-air arm that would interlock with the American sea-air arm.

This, so far as it went, was a pretty harsh dose for the French, the Belgians and the like. It was not, however, so far as it went, total isolationism in any recognizable form—except isolationism from the Continent of Europe. For Taft's final island concept took in much of Asia as areas to be held.

13

"SOFT" IN EUROPE;
"HARD" IN ASIA

The most fascinating of all the questions raised by Robert A. Taft in his various attitudes in world affairs was this question: Why was he so hesitant about anything resembling American intervention in Europe and so advanced, some of the time, in his demands for harder and harder actions against the Communists in Asia?

To attempt any answer one can rely in part on what he knows but he must go also into a good deal of sheer speculation. There was a great complex of known and suspected factors, some of which went back to hardy roots, like the long struggle in this country, beginning with Pearl Harbor, as to where the main effort should be made in a two-ocean war.

The orthodox, Midwest-based Republican party, that is, Taft's party, was from the start preoccupied with the Pacific. These Republicans had for the most part been identified with the America First movement, the intellectual headquarters of which was in Chicago. They had taken up a passionate belief that the United States could and should stay out of the war, and they had bitter and undying hostility toward those Eastern, internationalist Republicans typified by Henry L. Stimson, Franklin Roosevelt's Secretary of War, who were not only interventionist but unforgivably pro-British.

The Taft Republicans felt that if we *must* become involved we ought to fight an essentially national, as distinguished from an international or allied, war, and that we ought to do this in Asia. (Many of them disliked the term Far East, because it was a British term, though Taft himself would use it occasionally.)

The Japanese attack on Pearl Harbor ended a certain aspect of the debate (it was no longer possible to say that we could stay out of the war) but only one aspect. Mr. Roosevelt for many months afterward was under heavy pressure from the Taft Republicans to give top consideration to the struggle against Japan. This, of course, he threw off; he put the emphasis on the liberation of Europe and with Winston Churchill entered an Anglo-American association that saved both worlds. The decision seems now to have been strongly supported by the facts.

The industrial and fundamental warmaking power of Japan was, relative to what had been seized and put to work against us in Europe, simply piddling. Europe, moreover, was of course the ancestral home of the United States, apart from the fact that it was also the cradle of the only civilization that was really relevant to this country and to this century.

All these powerful arguments—and even the final, unanswerable argument after the fact that we never had even to engage the main body of Japanese troops in order to bring their empire to earth, though with the aid of the atom bomb —never impressed the Taft Republicans.

They took the view, and many of them to this day hold it, that Mr. Roosevelt had in some way tricked the United States into entering the war. This was an honest, if harsh, view and honest men put it forward then and now, perhaps because they were and are rightly aware that Mr. Roosevelt *was* far more belligerent after the 1940 elections than his campaign speeches had forecast. Nevertheless, the Taft Republicans in Congress pressed very far along this line.

They spent vast effort afterward in a strange, unlovely proceeding the meaning of which was to try to suggest that the Japanese had not really attacked us at Pearl Harbor after all—or that if they had, Mr. Roosevelt had simply bullied them into it. Almost they were willing to exculpate Tojo if only they could blame President Roosevelt; perhaps never before in history had so large and responsible a section of a great political party so attacked the honor of its own national government in prosecuting a war.

And in the meantime, the very nature of Mr. Roosevelt's grand strategy of Europe First led to the progressive elevation within the national war machine of the internationalist Republicans and a corresponding decline in the current national significance of the Taft Republicans. All those who made high martial policy—civilians and generals alike— were more or less pro-Europe. It is probable that it was at this early point that General George C. Marshall, who was then Army Chief of Staff, fell into disfavor with Taft.

The position, therefore, was this: The Taft Republicans

felt that their counsel had been rejected out of hand and that we had got into a war we need not have fought. They felt that once in we had, again by the rejection of their counsel, gone about it the wrong way and had been taken in by the British. And finally they felt that uncharacteristic and therefore unworthy Republicans had reached undue place and power.

Just as the Roosevelt decision to fight first for Europe had been successful beyond logical challenge when one looked at the result, so it fell out that the postwar Truman anti-Communist policies in Europe had visibly checked the Kremlin in the area of the Mediterranean and perhaps even in France.

And, on the other side, it could not be sensibly denied that the free world had at the same time suffered a great blow in the fall of China to the Communists—whether Generalissimo Chiang Kai-shek jumped, as the Democrats tended to claim, or was pushed by Roosevelt-Truman, as Taft's people always argued. No matter how one looked at it, it had to be acknowledged that American policy in China had failed to the extent that this policy was to contain communism.

It thus came about that both by conviction and by the necessities of political partisanship Taft turned more and more to Asia in his complaints against the Democrats. This was the place to turn to, if for no other reason than the fact that Truman had demonstrably done a fine job in Europe, both with the Marshall Plan and with the famous doctrine that was the salvation of Greece and Turkey. Recriminations would not readily lie in this area of Democratic policy—for it was *Democratic* policy, though with much Republican help, and Taft was honest enough to acknowledge that fact.

All this is not to suggest that he consciously put partisanship above every other consideration; it is nevertheless a fact that he came very close to doing just this unconsciously or subconsciously and on many occasions.

Accordingly, by 1948 Taft was taking a leading place in the development of an orthodox Republican accusatory issue, the substance of which was that first Roosevelt and then Truman had deliberately promoted the China Communists at the expense of Chiang's Nationalists.

"Today in China," Taft observed in Congress on February 24, 1948, "we continue a policy which threatens to undo in the Far East everything the Marshall Plan is trying to do in Western Europe.

"From the beginning we have encouraged the Chinese Communists. . . . Unless vigorous action is taken immediately all Manchuria will be lost to Communism. If Communism dominates Manchuria, how can we hope that in future years we will be able to keep it out of Japan?

"The practicability of rehabilitation for China and the value of relief is open to question, but certainly we can provide the Chinese (Nationalist) Government with the arms and ammunition necessary to resist Communist forces in Manchuria as we have undertaken to resist them in Greece. . . .

"*I believe very strongly that the Far East is ultimately even more important to our future peace than is Europe.*" (Italics mine.)

There was the beginning here of another Taft inconsistency, for in 1951 in his book, *A Foreign Policy for Americans*, he declared: "It has been suggested that there is a fundamental issue between those who think that Europe is more important and those who think that Asia is more important. *Certainly my position is not an extreme one on Asia. I only insist that we apply to Asia the same basic policy which we apply to Europe.*" (Italics mine.)

Speaking generally, however, Taft clearly and for most of the time put the Asian priority far higher. By 1950 he was saying in Congress that there was no longer "the slightest doubt" that a "sincere aid" to Chiang would have stopped the Chinese Communists, but in the same passage he was able for the moment to take a quite untypical position that for once was almost in agreement with Dean Acheson.

"In recent months," he said, "it has of course been very doubtful whether aid to the Nationalist Government could be effective, and no one desires to waste American efforts." He even held open, at that time, the possibility of eventual American recognition of the Chinese Communist regime, saying, "We can determine later whether we ever wish to recognize the Chinese Communists and what the ultimate disposition of Formosa (the Chinese Nationalist island refuge) shall be."

Again and again Taft's attitude in Asia was one alternately of action and of withdrawal. Though he endlessly denounced the Democrats for not having effectively helped Chiang, his own recommendations for subsequent aid to the Nationalists were sometimes at variance in form or spirit with each other.

Though he had argued, as to Europe, that sending military supplies to Britain for use against the Nazis was unconscionable intervention, there is this passage in David Lawrence's highly competent magazine *U.S. News and World Report* of a Taft interview of March, 1952:

"*Q.* If Communist China attacked Indo-China, would you favor going to war with China over that?"

"*A.* Yes, I would, but not with American land troops. We are at war with Communist China today. . . . We are already arming the French and their Indo-Chinese allies. I would arm Chiang Kai-shek's troops, as I said the other day. I think we ought to arm them now and have them ready to enter that war, if it comes."

"*Q.* Wouldn't you be afraid that you would drag Russia into the war?"

"*A.* Absolutely not . . . What does Russia care about *a local war* with Communist China?" (Italics mine.)

"*Q.* Russia has a treaty with Communist China."

"*A.* But Communist China is perhaps 7,000 miles away from Moscow. There's no threat to Russia in a civil war in South China."

"*Q.* Wasn't that the basis for the policy we adopted (in the Korean war) of not bombing bases in Manchuria?"

"*A.* That was one explanation given by the (Truman) Administration. I always thought it was hokum."

"*Q.* What was their real reason . . . ?"

"*A.* I can't tell you, but I think that part of it is that they didn't want to offend Great Britain. They were afraid that an all-out war with Communist China would involve a serious problem. . . . I never thought that bombing Manchuria or use of Chiang's troops would in any way bring Russia into the war. But the other thing that (General) MacArthur proposed, the complete blockade of Communist China, would have gotten us in pretty serious difficulty with the British at Hong Kong."

Taft's position on the Korean war changed much and often. Just after Truman had gone to the aid of the South Korean victims of Communist North Korea's assault in June of 1950, the Senator basically approved the meaning of the President's action, which he was later to call "Truman's war" and an "unnecessary war."

"No one can deny," he told the Senate on June 28, 1950, "that a serious crisis exists. . . . Without question the attack of the North Koreans is an outrageous act of aggression. . . .

"The President's statement of policy represents a complete change in the programs and policies heretofore proclaimed by the Administration. . . . *It seems to me that the time had to come, sooner or later, when we would give definite notice to the Communists that a move beyond a declared line would result in war.* [Italics mine.]

"This has been the policy which we have adopted in Europe. Whether the President has chosen the right time or right place to declare this policy may be open to question. . . .

"The entire unfortunate crisis has been produced, first by

the outrageous aggressive attitude of Soviet Russia and second by the bungling and inconsistent foreign policy of the Administration.

"I have not thoroughly investigated the question of the right and power of the President to do what he has done. His action unquestionably has brought about a de facto war. He has brought that war about without consulting Congress and without Congressional approval. . . . So far as I can see . . . I would say that there is no authority to use armed forces in support of the United Nations in the absence of some previous action by Congress dealing with the subject and outlining the general circumstances and the amount of the forces that can be used."

While Taft was sharp with the President in such passages, his attitude at the time was generally viewed as fundamentally approving the fact, if not the form, of the intervention. Washington dispatches of the period spoke of the extraordinary unity the President had now achieved on an issue of foreign policy. Taft's speech was welcomed by the internationalists; they felt that, for him, it was remarkably soft toward the President and toward the whole enterprise.

But all this had changed by 1951. In October of that year, Taft told a Republican banquet in Detroit: "We could have no more tragic example of the results of wavering and weakness than the Korean war. It was an unnecessary war which could have been prevented by common sense and a planned program against Communism."

Where, now, was the Taft approval of 1950 of the theory that "the time had to come, sooner or later, when we would give definite notice to the Communists that a move beyond a declared line would result in war"?

Perhaps there was nothing in this case in the way of an established inconsistency but to ordinary minds it certainly looked a good deal like one in spirit. For what in June of 1950 had been "open to question"—that is, whether Mr. Truman had selected the right time and place to draw his line against Communist aggression—had become in October of 1951 beyond any question at all. It had become, flatly, an "unnecessary war." For, in 1951 Taft went on: "Today we find ourselves in Korea exactly where we were three years ago and face exactly the same problems except that there have been more than 85,000 deaths and woundings of American boys, the loss of a million South Koreans, the utter destruction of the very country we undertook to defend, and the waste of billions of dollars.

"The Korean war was begun by President Truman without the slightest authority from Congress or the people. . . . It is said that we had to go into Korea under the United Nations Charter to punish international military aggression. That was for Congress to decide. But if that was the purpose it has utterly failed today, for the United Nations has refused to punish Communist China, though the Chinese aggression was far more serious and directed at the United Nations itself. The only principle we have established is that if the aggressor is big enough he will not be punished."

In his book of 1951, he observed: "We went into Korea on the theory that the United Nations was going to punish aggression in order to prevent aggression in the future. I think it is a sound principle, if you have an international organization with ability to do the job. The difficulty is that we were relying on a weak reed in the United Nations. We went in with the possibility facing us that there might be further aggression and *knowing that we could not rely on the United Nations.* [Italics mine]. We were successful in defeating the North Koreans but . . . we were attacked by the Chinese. We had been sucked into something that was more than we could undertake and we found ourselves in an extremely unfortunate position.

"Once it became apparent that the policy of punishing aggression could not be carried through there was some logical argument for entirely evacuating Korea. But having gone into Korea, having suffered more than a hundred thousand casualties . . . there seemed to be no choice except to see it through.

"Since it was impossible to invade China, the best solution would have been to drive the Chinese out of Korea, to ask the United Nations to set up a Korean Republic, to maintain our troops there for some time to come and then arm the Koreans with weapons which would enable them to stand against Chinese attack, and to give them such economic and arms aid in peace and military aid from the sea and air in war as we might be able to afford.

". . . Regardless of the matter of an armistice (in Korea) if we really believe in a policy of containing Communism there is no logical reason why we should not give a hundred per cent support to the Chinese Nationalist Government on

Formosa and reject any idea whatever of a compromise in this issue."

So what was the meaning óf Taft on Asia? The man who had felt that the Nazis never threatened American security and that it was folly to extend military aid to Britain now felt that holding the island of Formosa in 1951 was far more important than had been holding the island of England, the birthplace of his race and of the liberties that he so loved, in 1941.

Why? Perhaps, most of all, because Taft never feared fascism as he feared communism. The first, he thought, lacked the appeal of the second to the faceless hordes of ordinary men that he always faintly feared and never understood.

And there was more to it. The *politico*-military cult that developed around General MacArthur, with Taft's powerful assistance, represented far more than an uncritical and excessive adulation for a great and articulate military leader who was, for all that, not really the only one developed by the United States in the decade 1940–1950. (A man named Omar Bradley, for instance, probably had successfully commanded in heavy action in France more men than General MacArthur commanded together in the whole of his long career.)

The Asian cult was, in fact, almost mystically based, and one gets onto a sticky terrain in attempting to describe how it could come to dominate the whole Taft wing of the Republican party, to a greater extent than it dominated Taft himself. It rested most of all, one thinks, on a strong concept of American nationalism; on long inherited suspicion of the British; on a wish, conscious or not, to have this country go it alone; on an attitude of rejection toward Europe. Taft himself, though he adopted some of General MacArthur's disputed military policies for Asia, sensed and was not always wholly comfortable in the cult aspect of the thing.

I asked him shortly before the 1952 Republican Presidential Convention whether General MacArthur might not become, because of the comparative identity of the Taft-MacArthur views on the Orient, a serious rival to his own ambitions.

"I think not," said Taft, with an access of dry objectivity. "If the convention is displeased with the heat of the Taft frying pan, can you see it accepting the MacArthur fire?"

IV.

THE LAST, BEST TAFT

☆ 14 ☆

THE DEFEAT THAT LED TO
THE VICTORY

R obert A. Taft went in 1952 to Chicago in great strength
for what he knew would be his last attempt at the
Republican Presidential nomination, barring a future possible
renomination if he should reach the White House. Now
Chicago became the place of his last defeat—and the place
also from which he emerged upon reflection to his last and
greatest victory, a victory over most of his indomitable
prejudices that was to permit him at last to become the
statesman that he had never quite been before.

In July of 1952 the heat in Chicago was all but unbearable; it reached 110 degrees in the working press rooms below the stockyards amphitheater. And the bitterness of the
Twenty-fifth Republican National Convention had not been
matched for forty years. In 1912, Bob Taft's father, President
William Howard Taft, had gone to this same city of Chicago
determined to smash the pretensions of a more popular and
more liberal but less *Republican* challenger called Theodore
Roosevelt.

Bob Taft went there in 1952 in determination to smash
the pretensions of a more popular and relatively more liberal
but less *Republican* challenger, Dwight D. Eisenhower. The

171

father and his managers had held the party machinery in iron grip; so did the son forty years later. Like father, like son.

Both times the party machinery was ruthlessly used by Taftites. The first time, in the case of William Howard Taft, the orthodox drove Theodore Roosevelt from the convention hall—but in the autumn the Republican party lost to Woodrow Wilson and the Democrats. For Theodore Roosevelt, crying "burglar . . . piracy . . . naked theft . . ." went out on a third party ticket, the Bull Moose, and the GOP was never again to be the same.

Bob Taft, the loser at Chicago in 1952 to General Eisenhower, could not conceivably have emulated Theodore Roosevelt, even had he an equivalent right to feel morally outraged—as he didn't. Nor could William Howard Taft, had it come to that. Like father, like son.

Robert Taft's forces gathered at Chicago with about 530 committed or pledged votes, and 604 would have chosen him as the Republican candidate for President of the United States. But the whole story of the convention came down to this: He could not have been nominated except with the aid of tainted ballots. In the South—an old Taft family political fief—the Taft managers had strong-armed the Eisenhower people as nobody had been strong-armed since Howard Taft's people had given the treatment to Theodore Roosevelt's people four decades before. This was not the whole story in 1952—it had quite another side and political moralism was not really the whole issue at Chicago—but for the moment it is enough.

The proper control of seventy-two delegates—whether they ought to belong to Howard Taft or to Theodore Roosevelt—was at issue in 1912. The proper control of sixty-eight delegates—whether they ought to belong to Bob Taft or to Dwight Eisenhower—was at issue in 1952.

It was in 1912 that the term "steam roller" was first applied, by Clark Grier, a Roosevelt delegate from Georgia, to a political operation, that of the William Howard Taft forces. So remorselessly did it roll that Senator Depew of New York commented sourly: "It is only a question now which corpse gets the most flowers."

The 1952 Robert A. Taft model of the steam roller was formidable; but in the end it did not roll, and what Depew had called the corpses were in this case the broken Taft delegations.

To understand the 1952 convention it is necessary first to go back to the atmosphere of the time. Taft had by now become *the* Republican of the United States, in any ordinary and orthodox sense of that term and in any sense of past achievement.

General Eisenhower, possibly because of his liberal foreign policy views and his long association with the Democratic Presidents Franklin Roosevelt and Harry Truman, had been considered by many acute politicians to be actually a Democrat if one scratched him deeply enough. There was the strongest suspicion that even Harry S. Truman, who had an instinct for a fellow partisan, held this view of the General's political heart.

For four years Taft and his partisans had been trumpeting

about the country the charge that the Republicans had lost in 1948 only because they allowed the blandishments of the Deweyites to nominate that figure of anathema to Taft, "a me-too man." Moreover, it was the Republicans of *Congress,* in which Taft of course was dominant, who alone had made a consistent national demonstration against the Truman administration. And it was the Republicans in Congress who almost alone had found and developed the national issues upon which it was proposed to fight the Democrats—"corruption, Communism and cronyism," as the Taftites described the case.

Again, and it was plainly the truth, the Midwestern or Congressional Republicans had opened the way to victory. Again, as it turned out, they were to be denied the opportunity to exploit this way with one of their own.

Eisenhower, for his part, had refused to become a candidate in any active sense. Taft's people for more than a year had been walking their well-worn paths in the states to gather up delegates for 1952—and incidentally making their characteristic mistake of making public claims on delegates in detail and thus opening themselves prematurely to the sharp counteraction of the forces headed by Taft's old and classical antagonist, Dewey of New York. Dewey, Senators Henry Cabot Lodge, Jr., of Massachusetts, James H. Duff of Pennsylvania and all the sleek, powerful Dewey apparatus were in the field in behalf of Eisenhower.

Taft had, as usual, a disorganized team of managers— Representative Clarence Brown of Ohio, Carroll Reece of Tennessee, David Ingalls of Ohio and Tom Coleman of Wisconsin. Though Reece lived in Tennessee he could only be called an "Ohio Republican"; he was the Southern Taft manager. Coleman therefore was the only outlander in the lot, but he was, of course, safely Midwestern.

Lodge, as the Eisenhower field manager, got word that the Taft people, who had utterly controlled the traditional and minute Republican organization in Texas in the past, were going to "steal" the Texas State Convention this time, because Johnny-Come-Lately Republicans were making alarming manifestations of interest in Eisenhower. The Eisenhower organization, the largest and richest by far ever thrown up in a Presidential year, began to "alert the press and radio," in the words of one of its leaders. The Texas State Republican convention at Mineral Wells was most fully covered, and what this coverage disclosed was not pretty.

A pro-Eisenhower faction headed by H. J. Porter of Houston had put on a tremendous campaign over the state and beyond fair question had beaten the pro-Taft people soundly in the precinct and county conventions. If it came down to a matter of the votes cast, General Eisenhower had clearly won the Republican delegation of thirty-eight from Texas.

But if it came down to a definition of who was a Republican, this was not so sure. While the pro-Taft Old Guard state organization at Mineral Wells was harshly and without the slightest dissimulation casting out pro-Eisenhower delegates, Taft's people raised the contention that the "Eisenhower Republicans" in Texas had been Democrats yesterday and no doubt would be again tomorrow. The Taft line was that the "Eisenhower Republicans" had gone into the primaries for the single purpose of knifing Taft.

Again, as was so often the case, the heart of the matter lay in an issue that it would be difficult for most people to be exact about: Who was a Republican? To Taft, of course, the answer was quite clear. A Republican was a Republican, not indispensably a man who had always been one, but at minimum a man who had been one for a respectable period of time.

By the time the Republican National Convention opened in Chicago, Texas had become almost the whole show. Taft's managers in the field had gone on to the end showing the least possible understanding of people and of publicity. They even opposed television coverage of the deliberations of the Republican National Committee on the issue of the competing pro-Taft and pro-Eisenhower slates from Texas. Of course, they earned, for themselves and for Taft, the epithet "star chamber."

At one point, Taft suggested, with an air of magnanimity, that Texas could be split evenly and General Eisenhower, who was a novice in this sort of political in-fighting, was quoted as saying, "Swell." But Lodge, who was to Dewey in this Stop-Taft enterprise about what General Omar Bradley had been in Normandy to Eisenhower at supreme headquarters, quickly caught and disarmed the unexploded grenade that Eisenhower had lightly dropped. It was a moral issue, said Lodge, and one did not compromise moral issues. It was on this point alone, he felt, that General Eisenhower could be nominated without question.

A kind of evangelistic fever swept Chicago; the Eisenhower men paraded about shaking at the Taft people signs that read: "Thou Shalt Not Steal." Taft himself, working twenty hours a day in his headquarters in the Conrad Hilton Hotel, blinked under this brandishing of the Commandment. He was not stunned; he was simply and wholly uncomprehending.

One has been informed reliably that all through the proceedings in Texas Taft had been kept abreast and that he held an ultimate responsibility for the Old Guard actions and decisions there that he never sought to disavow. Nevertheless, the whole Chicago proceeding had turned into one from which he instinctively fled. He was enormously uncomfortable in the face of any emotional display; and in this regard Chicago was at that time a great bath of emotion. And he had no genuine understanding of the *meaning* of what was afoot.

He had come to Chicago prepared to defend his general record and particularly his views of foreign policy; he recognized that it was *these* that really made him objectionable to so many powerful Eastern internationalist Republicans and independents. He felt therefore in the position of a commander who had prepared to withstand a siege against his capital and main airfield only to find that his enemies were driving against the peony beds in the public parks.

He knew, as did everyone at all familiar with politics, that Southern Republican delegates, speaking generally, had for nearly a century been in one candidate's pocket or another's —of late, mostly a Taft pocket. He did not have the faintest realization of the movement that had gone like a brush fire through Texas—a movement not simply to select General Eisenhower over Senator Taft but to elect Eisenhower to the Presidency. He did not feel at all immoral, this man who had been called all too respectable, and so he could not credit the accusation being so widely thrown about that Bob Taft had, so to speak, condoned a process of thievery. He simply did not understand any of it.

Accordingly, at the convention the divided Taft managers were driven into one untenable and absurdly inept position after another; they were put in the attitude of men cynically deriding what the Eisenhower people endlessly shouted, and with a good deal of justification, was only "fair play."

After much and bitter preliminary struggling at Chicago the question of Texas reached the convention floor. Nothing short of an unconditional surrender from the Taft people would have been accepted now by the Eisenhower managers—and even a tacit surrender they at length were strong enough, amid the exultant shouts of their followers, to refuse. For when desperate backstage consultations had led them nowhere, the Taft people went on the floor offering to concede that *sixty-one* of the sixty-eight disputed delegates should not be allowed to vote on their own or on other seating contests. The seven Louisianians were to be considered pure enough to vote on their own bona fides; the sixty-one Texans and Georgians were to stand aside.

"No," said the Eisenhower people. They put the issue to the floor and the Taft "compromise" was rejected 658 to

548. Not all who voted with the majority actually were against Taft as the ultimate nominee; some simply could not withstand the enormous pressure from a country that was coming to be convinced that Chicago was about to become the seat of an enormity of political villainies. This concept, though not exact, was not discouraged by Dewey, Lodge and the other Eisenhower men.

Taft was by this time aware that something had hit him very hard; but, again, he could not quite take it all in. He rallied his forces and tried in vain to suggest that political conventions were pretty grimly practical affairs and that perhaps the other side had not been in all respects a model of purity as this would be defined by a ladies' amateur political club. And because he knew these things about conventions he never quite grasped that others did not.

In all these circumstances the Eisenhower people—and back of them all was the redoubtable Dewey, calm, unflinching in his power—pushed massively on, and everywhere they were immeasurably helped by the continuing errors of the Taft backers. A Taft man from Illinois, Senator Everett M. Dirksen, made a gratuitous attack on Dewey, who had after all carried the Republican banners in two Presidential elections, and alienated many who had been emotionally at least on the fence.

Dewey, at the head of New York's delegation of ninety-six votes, had ninety-two of this great bloc in his pocket. The New York delegates had gone to Chicago with the most pointed possible reminders that Dewey controlled the patronage of that state and that any man who broke away and went for Taft would be cut off from all patronage within two days of the end of the convention.

The outcome of the Texas issue, therefore, was the breakthrough; it was Dewey who widened this into a powerful counteroffensive over the whole line, that destroyed the Taft candidacy. The first ballot, taking into account the switches of votes made as it progressed, brought for Taft the end. The result, before the switches, was Eisenhower 595, Taft 500, and a hundred-odd votes cast here and there. The "revised" first ballot, after the switches, was Eisenhower 845, Taft 280, with 81 votes here and there.

Taft retired to the silence in his headquarters in the Conrad Hilton, but the immediate response among the Old Guardists generally was a desperate bitterness, mingled with curses and tears. The curses were nearly all connected with one name: "Dewey." General Eisenhower reversed the usual procedure and went at once to call upon the vanquished Taft. There were boos for the General. The corridor at Taft headquarters was in a chaos; Taft workers wept.

Taft pressed his way calmly into the hall from his office. General Eisenhower looked shy and hesitant and some in the crowd set off a chant "We Want Taft." Taft, far the more self-possessed of the two men, stopped all this, at once.

"I came over to pay a call of friendship on a great American," said General Eisenhower. "His willingness to co-operate is absolutely necessary to the success of the Republican party in the campaign and of the Administration to follow."

"I want to congratulate General Eisenhower," said Taft. "I shall do everything possible in the campaign to secure his election and to help in his Administration."

This comment, it should be understood, was at the time a little on the pro forma side. While it would not have been possible for Taft ever to obstruct a national Republican ticket or to refuse it at least nominal support, he had suffered at Chicago a thrust that would have broken a less rocklike man.

Again he had seen, as it looked to him then, the triumph—and the definitely final one, so far as his own White House ambitions were concerned—of the Deweyites. He viewed what had happened at Chicago as the victory, through Dewey, of all that he had deplored and fought within the Republican party. It was significant, at this end of the convention as it had been all the way through, that Taft's people *never* denounced his antagonist, Eisenhower, but *always* denounced Dewey and those who had long been close to Dewey. Eisenhower to them was only the hammer in the hands of Dewey.

And there were, moreover, forces at work within the Taft camp that even Taft could not have wholly controlled. Prominent Taft men were heard to say at Chicago that they would give only the barest minimum help or none at all in the coming campaign; the Taftites felt that the convention's result was the end of their every dream and that the party had again been kidnapped by non-Republicans.

So strong was this feeling that Lodge, running in the fall for re-election in Massachusetts, was openly set upon by large groups of influential Taft men—a circumstance that materially contributed to the victory of his Democratic opponent, John F. Kennedy, but a circumstance for which Lodge himself rightly never blamed Taft personally. Here again, in the last analysis, *any* Republican was in Taft's view better than *any* Democrat. He did not take part in the Massachusetts campaign, and indeed no ordinary rule of politics would have required this, but he did upon solicitation send a letter to a Taft man in Massachusetts saying that Lodge ought to be returned for the good of the party.

Finally, after the debacle of Chicago in 1952, Taft, before going off to Murray Bay in Canada to ponder many things, did what anyone who knew him would have supposed he would do. He prepared a manifesto for private circulation among his closest associates taking full personal responsibility for all that had happened to his campaign, at and before Chicago, and admonishing them to have tolerance for each other and to avoid recriminations. He could have done no other; he was the boss in victory, he was the boss in defeat. He was willing to take credit for the sunshine; he did not shrink the blame when it rained.

To attempt to pass judgment on his defeat is a hard and perhaps a presumptuous task. As one onlooker, my own view of the business was this: Taft *had* to be rejected if the historic movement of the Republican party toward liberalism and internationalism was to continue, whether or not he had to be defeated in order that the party could win in November.

The "moral issue" was profoundly useful—it may be that

it was indispensable, though this is doubtful—to this defeat. But it was, nevertheless, only the *method* by which Taft was defeated, and not the *reason*. The reason underlying all else was in two parts. Taft in his period of irresponsibility had morally shocked too many people of great power; and Taft on foreign policy had frightened beyond recall too many of the same. He had to fall, because history was moving against him.

☆ 15 ☆

MORNINGSIDE "SURRENDER"

Taft had left the 1952 Presidential convention confronting a private moral and intellectual crisis. At sixty-two years of age he was prepared to contemplate, at least, the unthinkable. He was prepared for the first time in his life to consider the possibility of offering only remote, qualified support to the institution that to more than any other on earth he had given his devotion, the Republican party.

His last defeat for the Presidential nomination had been tragic to him in the most exquisite meaning of a word that because it was an extreme word he used only rarely and advisedly. The final rejection had been to him not simply a *final* rejection of Taft but a rejection of the earnest, brave, lost exertions of millions of men and women who since the time of Abraham Lincoln had suffered much to build and to keep alive a great political instrumentality. This instrumentality, he now thought, had been all but destroyed—destroyed by the unworthy animosities and ambitions of others (these were, of course, "the Dewey people") and only for the purpose of putting forward as a Presidential nominee a man who had merited nothing in that line of endeavor and who was, in the political sense, a man nobody really knew. (Another distinguished politician once told me of General

Eisenhower: "He won't do; wrong business for him." This was close to Taft's own view of the case.)

The surface manifestations at the Chicago convention—the taunting yells of the winners as the bunting came down and Taft's loyal, not too competent people once more staggered from the field in the exhaustion of failure—had been hard enough to bear. But infinitely worse was Taft's first estimate of the extent and ultimate meaning of the disaster.

He saw in General Eisenhower still another "me-too" candidate; he looked sadly forward to another campaign in which he supposed the despised Democrats would again find an exasperatingly illogical unity and would again go forward to victory in November.

As he took stock of the past, it looked to him that the guardians and the sons of the founders of the party perhaps had lost it for good and that now though there would be a good deal of windy nonsense about two parties there would really be only one party, no matter who was elected. Recalling his own record and the records of those about him it seemed to him that he had been finally and irretrievably defrauded—and defrauded precisely *because* he had earned what he has sought—and that they would now be punished for having helped him to earn it.

His strong paternalistic sense was quite as outraged at the second point as at the first: Taft could bear his own disappointments better than he could bear the disappointments of those others who had done what he told them to do when he told them to do it.

He went away to the old Taft family summer place in

Murray Bay, Quebec, in an attitude that in a less decent and less honorably wounded man could have been called a sulking attitude. At Murray Bay he entered the impenetrable silence —a silence the significance of which was soon to begin to bear in upon the politicians who were by this time setting up General Eisenhower's campaign headquarters in the Commodore Hotel in New York.

Taft in Canada was thinking deeply, even for him; battling within him were the anger and the sense of loss against the lifelong concept of loyalty to the Organization. It may be that left alone he might indeed have taken the almost inconceivable decision more or less to sit out the campaign. But Taft was not left alone, and his broodings did not long remain only his own.

An old Taft journalistic friend, Edwin Lahey of the Chicago *Daily News,* went up to Murray Bay, sought out Taft, and shortly sent to the outside world an ominous dispatch that opened: "General Eisenhower's chances of winning the support of Senator Taft of Ohio (meaning for the campaign) are about zero." Lahey went on to stipulate the conditions under which this support would be forthcoming and the first of these was that there must be no reprisals in the new Republican Administration, if it was to be chosen by the voters against Taft men.

"Senator Taft," Lahey reported, "also wants some assurances from General Eisenhower that the nominee is not going to repudiate the Taft-Hartley Act, even by indirection. *And finally Senator Taft would like to see General Eisenhower talking like a Republican and acting like a man running for President.*

"Many of these assurances Senator Taft would want in writing."

Plainly, all this had come from Taft himself, though Lahey was at pains to take personal responsibility for all that was said in the dispatch. The news was put under careful examination in the Commodore, along with a good many less public bulletins on the subject. The result was this: General Eisenhower invited Taft, who had not himself lifted a finger for such a consultation, to come to New York to see him.

This was the way in which was arranged the celebrated Morningside Heights Conference of September 12, 1952.

Taft arrived at Morningside with a long statement (it will be recalled that Lahey had spoken of matters "in writing"). This document, though it had been read in advance by Senator Frank Carlson of Kansas, an Eisenhower man, was not actually seen by the General himself until the very morning of the confrontation.

In substance it was a proud manifesto and an apologia for nearly all that Taft and the other orthodox Republicans had stood. Its tone hardly escaped belligerence, as Taft's manner of delivering it hardly escaped the manner of a quiet ultimatum. When Taft and General Eisenhower had finished a breakfast of two hours they were "in full agreement," as it was said at the time. And they were "in full agreement" on exactly the statement, barring inconsequential changes, that Taft alone had prepared and taken into the General's home at Columbia University. Taft, it was stated, would now go all the way for Eisenhower in the campaign.

Some of the more advanced Eastern internationalists among the Eisenhower men privately and angrily deplored the incident, and especially the fact that in two hours of discussion General Eisenhower had in effect put his initials on a profoundly important paper of which the only author was Taft.

Some even called it "the Surrender of Morningside Heights," but they were right only if one chose to disregard the fact that the second of the two powerful conferees was not and never had been the "either-or" man that Taft had always been. General Eisenhower was a flexible man; before this he had dealt with brilliant and dedicated men to whom nearly everything was principle and little was negotiable detail. The mind cannot cope with the thought of such a meeting in reverse circumstances; of Taft receiving and accepting the terms of a defeated adversary.

But General Eisenhower's determination had been unalterable from the first. It was to *make* Taft like him, if this was at all possible, and in any event to placate Taft and to bring him into the campaign and then into the grand designs that the Republicans proposed to raise after the election. Eisenhower was concerned to preserve a combat effective in Taft.

It was, in short, a "surrender" by the Eisenhower people to the extent that through him they had accepted Taft's text, chapter and verse.

The General was magnanimous; the statement given out

with his concurrence at Morningside by Taft fully vindicated the predictions that some things would have to be "in writing." It was all "in writing," and it was all Taft. And the manner of its issuance was also Taft's; it all had the bony candor that was a part of him.

"I have never," he said, "changed my intention expressed at Chicago [that is to do all 'possible' for the Eisenhower ticket] but of course I have not intended to abandon in any way the principles I have fought for for the past fourteen years or abandon those countless friends who supported me in the preconvention campaign.

"I have felt, therefore, that I could be far more effective in the campaign if I could state to the people, after talking to General Eisenhower, my definite convictions regarding the character of his Administration when he is elected and the principles by which it will be guided.

"A good many of my friends have been concerned because so many of his [Eisenhower's] editorial and columnist supporters, and other individuals who have heretofore always taken the New Deal line, have been urging him to repudiate the Republican platform, approve New Deal policies and purge everyone who has fought hard for Republican principles against Truman and Acheson and the rest of the left-wingers.

"I have felt confident that General Eisenhower has no such intention. The expression of such a confidence can be far more effective after a personal talk with him."

Taft went on, then, to state his own views in detail—views which he said Eisenhower had accepted—that the issue was "liberty against creeping socialization," and that "the new Administration" would protect this liberty against the Democrats.

"After a satisfactory discussion with General Eisenhower this morning for two hours," he added, "I am satisfied that this is his philosophy. I am convinced that he will carry out the pledges of the Republican platform. . . . I am convinced that General Eisenhower believes in the words and spirit of the statement of Republican principles and objectives adopted by Republican members of Congress Feb. 6. . . .

"I cannot say that I agree with all of General Eisenhower's views on the foreign policy to be pursued in Europe and the rest of the world, but I think it is fair to say that our differences are differences of degree. . . . General Eisenhower emphatically agrees with me in the proposal to reduce drastically over-all expenses. . . . General Eisenhower has also told me that he believes strongly in our system of Constitutional limitations on Government power and that he abhors the left-wing theory that the Executive had unlimited power. . . .

"General Eisenhower has also told me that he believes in the basic principles of the Taft-Hartley Law, its protection of the people and the freedom of the union members themselves against the arbitrary use of power by big business or big labor, and is opposed to its repeal. . . .

"General Eisenhower agrees that the proper role of the Federal Government beyond its present activities is one of advice, research and assistance to the states, the local communities and the people.

"I have been concerned about the attitude of those who apparently are urging that we should eliminate from all activity many of those who have been the most active workers for Republican principles over recent years, and who make up at least one-half of the Republican party. General Eisenhower stated that in the making of appointments at high levels or low levels there will be no discrimination against anyone because he or she has supported me, and that he is determined to maintain the unity of the entire party by taking counsel with all factions and points of view.

"I am completed satisfied that General Eisenhower will give the country an Administration inspired by the Republican principles of continued and expanding liberty for all as against the continued growth of New Deal socialism which we would suffer under Governor Stevenson (the Democratic Presidential candidate), a representative of the left-wingers if not a left-winger himself.

"I urge all Americans and particularly those who have confidence in my judgment and my principles to vote for Eisenhower and Nixon, for all the Republican senatorial candidates and all the Republican House candidates and to do everything possible to bring many others to the polls to do the same."

The meaning of all this to Taft was deep—and well it might have been. It cast away from him the dreadful specter that he might have to take an unexampled and un-Taftian line toward the Republican ticket, one amounting to the cold shoulder. It gave him a reason for believing that all his past exertions had not been in vain. It permitted him, this man

who in the past had been able to accept defeats for himself
that he could not accept for the orthodox Republicans, to
believe that Chicago had not after all been a final defeat for
these orthodox. It gave him, in short, a reason for being. He
was now ready to go forth to do great battle for Eisenhower
and Nixon—not for them, really, but for the Republican
party, in which, as he saw it, not all was lost after all.

The newly reorganized Republican National Committee,
though now it had an Eisenhower and not a Taft complexion,
began to make many overtures to "Mr. Republican." General
Eisenhower's more intimate associates, among them "Young
Jim" Hagerty, who was later to become the President's press
officer in the White House, worked urgently and in every
way to pay to Taft honors that were hardly precedented for
a man in his position in the history of politics.

Taft's decision to go along, once made, was wholehearted,
and it came not a minute too soon. Those political correspondents who had set out shortly after the convention on
early tours of political soundings were unanimous in one
finding: The Taft Old Guard throughout the country was
bruised and sore and entirely uninterested in General Eisenhower until the signal came to them that Eisenhower and
Taft had made their accommodation.

The Old Guardists, though still distrustful of General
Eisenhower and still full of the bitterest memories concern-
ing "the Dewey people," to some extent now opened their
hearts to General Eisenhower—and to a very great extent
their capacious pockets. They comforted themselves by their
conviction that Taft in any case had not let them down, nor

had he let Eisenhower become an unfettered candidate. In a sense, they were quite right about this, even though it was to turn out that they were right perhaps more in an academic than in a practical way.

It is unquestionably true that the Eisenhower campaign bore the unmistakable stamp of Taft—and nowhere more than in the General's refusal to make any issue against any Republican anywhere for any reason, not even excluding Republicans who had traduced his old military mentor, General Marshall. This decision, that no "orthodox" Republican could be wrong, and certainly not in a campaign year, was Taftian to the core; it was precisely this thinking that had permitted Taft to support the McCarthys of the party.

But the important thing about Morningside and all that flowed from it was this. It formed a strange, powerful alliance, that so long as it survived could only be for the country's good, between two profoundly different men. And it enabled Taft for the first time to suspect that not everything done by the Eastern Republicans was necessarily and everywhere wrong. It formed, in a phrase that the President found more to his liking than did Taft, "a team." And more importantly it forced for a time, more or less against Taft's will and definitely against the habits of a political lifetime, an uneasy association between the two Republican parties— the party that Dewey had typified and the party that Taft had personified.

It was not that Taft ever consciously compromised anything; it was simply that events with which he was connected themselves operated toward compromise. To the end of his life the Morningside Heights document was a comfort to him; he could look back upon it as commemorating a place where he had pulled forth a certain kind of victory from defeat.

To him the victory was unquestioned because *he* never had the slightest doubt that Eisenhower had indeed "surrendered." In his mind he had brought from Morningside a paper validating the claims *and policies* of the orthodox Republicans as surely as the barons had wrested their charter from King John at Runnymede. To him the Manifesto of Morningside meant precisely what it said; and what it said was pretty plain.

It said that but for foreign policy (and even here the divergence was to be one only of "degree") the Eisenhower policies would be primarily the policies that Robert A. Taft had shaped and largely made.

16

THE SENATE MAN

It might almost be said that the institution of the United States Senate had been created for Robert A. Taft, or men like him, and he for it. Without it he could not have been the man he was; without him it will not soon be the same again. For here was a perfect meeting between a great parliamentarian and what, in one man's view at least, is the greatest parliamentary body the world has known.

The American parliament is a vastly different thing from the British one and Taft was of course a vastly different man from Winston Churchill; nevertheless he bestrode the one as surely as Churchill bestrode the other. They were, each in his very separate way, the two outstanding parliamentary men of their generation; the shy, dry solitary Taft, with his embodiment of so much of the Puritan tradition, and the grandly bibulous Churchill with his embodiment of so much of the Cavalier tradition. It is not surprising that they found so many things on which to disagree.

Though for fifteen years Taft moved in and out of a position of a relative, and at best a never decisive, power in the United States and in the Republican party, his influence on the American Congress within those years was matchless. The very qualities that always denied him success in national enterprises made possible and ever increased his success in Congress and particularly in its dominant branch, the Senate.

It will be readily recalled that for half a generation until the arrival of the Eisenhower Administration, whose essential political purposes are even yet not entirely clear, the White House was in the tenancy of men whose purpose was to make America over. What is perhaps not so readily recalled is that while these men accomplished much of what they sought, many of their plans were lost and defeated in a single place, the Senate of the United States.

The recent history of the Presidency—again necessarily excepting the present Presidency, upon whose designs time is yet to cast an adequate light—has been a movement toward the political enrichment of vast economic, social and voting groups in the United States.

The recent history of the Congress has been a history of resistance, not always total, not always successful, but resistance nevertheless, to an enlargement of Federal-popular power at the expense of the concept of states' rights or perquisites, however absurdly "states' rights" may have been overstated from time to time.

If one sought to identify above all others the Man of the Resistance one would have to settle upon Taft. It was he, more than any other, who forever clamored for and sometimes actually secured that recognition of the rights of Congress that the strong executive departments of Roosevelt and Truman extended only grudgingly and under duress.

And when it comes to that it was Taft who most of all

dragged from a reluctant and more or less uncaring public
a respect for him as a symbol of a political instrumentality,
Congress, that had generally and vastly declined in public
respect during the crisis years from the Great Depression to
the Second World War. These were nowhere good days for
legislative bodies. The terrible, thrusting problems of these
times led men everywhere to put their trust in some form of
quick *managerial* government as distinguished from the
despised "debating societies" with which to this day all
deliberative bodies, including the United Nations, are often
equated.

Taft's mind *was*, in this sense, perhaps "the best eighteenth-century mind in the Senate." As he preferred the
eighteenth-century concept of warfare, he preferred the
eighteenth-century notion of parliamentary government.

Much of the whole meaning of his political life was bound
up in the fact that his circumstances permitted him to in-
dulge this concept from the sanctuary of his seat in the
Senate, which was in the gift of a single state and could be
withdrawn by none other. It is possible, in the Senate, to
have an almost incredible power over the fortunes of this
country and to be quite beyond the reach of that country's
voters. (One might look, as an example, at a Senator McCarran of Nevada, who is sent to Washington by fewer voters
than live in a single typical election district in Manhattan
but in the McCarran Act has altered the whole immigration
policy of an immigrant nation.)

Taft had this power, at its highest peak, *because* he was
the kind of man who could be three times rejected by the

national Republican party. As in the party's conventions he represented always the lost hopes and thoughts of a great part of his party, always in the Senate he represented the highest interests of a political conservatism that was here dominant and to which he was indispensable. To have altered his views to the extent necessary to make him palatable to a national political convention would have been to lose much of his inherent power in the Senate. Had he won the Presidency by this method he would have lost decisively in Senate influence.

For the Congress, and the Senate in particular, have for a long time been controlled, in each party, precisely by the kind of men who cannot win Presidential nominations, and by strong presumption could not win a national election. The Democratic party in both Houses is and long has been in the grip of Southern Democrats who no more typify the national Democratic party than the long file of Taft-Republican committee chairmen typifies either the national Republican party generally or its present leader, General Eisenhower, specifically.

In the present Congress, at least seventy per cent of the Republican power is in the hands of men who were never really pro-Eisenhower until his nomination and election had become unarguable facts. In the last Democratic Congress, the Eighty-second, at least seventy per cent of the Democratic power was in hands of men who were never really pro-Truman. There is, therefore, a split personality; no party that wins a Presidential election is necessarily in control of the country, nor is that part of the party which selects the

Presidential candidate necessarily in control of the party itself in Congress.

This was true in all of Taft's life in the Senate. For fifteen years the Senate Republicans were for the most part Taft Republicans—that is, the authentically old-fashioned partisan article. The voice of their chief was in the legislative sense stronger than any voice that could be raised by that type of Republican who had controlled every party convention since 1936. It was stronger, moreover, even in Democratic Congresses than any single Democratic voice that spoke for either wing of the Democratic party, that is, the Southern-dominated Congressional wing or the Northern-dominated White House wing.

And it is only in the Senate that modern conditions still give hospitality to the political individualist. Here there is still a respectful hearing for the wrong-headed, the skeptic, the obstructionist, the transparent defamer, the shouter for vehement minorities of every kind—and also for a man like Taft, a legislative artist who worked always at his best when alone.

The Senate, in short, has changed very little in the century and a half since its creation. It still represents an aggregation of *states*, and only secondarily the voters, and it reflects the national mood of the past far more than of the present.

Committee chairmanships flowing from seniority, or Senate influence otherwise obtained—and Taft was greatly influential long before he was ever a Senate committee chairman—bring a power of checkmate and veto before which the strongest White House or the strongest public opinion must often stand hesitant. A Borah from a remote, lightly populated state like Idaho became, as chairman of the Senate Foreign Relations Committee, a negative voice in foreign policy equal to and sometimes even heard above that of the President of the United States.

It is not too hard to see how Taft would fit so ideally into the Senate. It is, above all, not an administrative organism—and administrative skill was never his long suit. It is an organism in which members may with considerable liberty choose between various forms of tasks, and bear down most on those tasks that suit them most. Taft's strongest point always was his immense ability at concentrating—whether in an abstract or a practical way made not the slightest difference to him—on political and legislative problems. Many a night he sat very late in a third-floor room in his house in the Georgetown section of Washington analyzing such a problem for the sheer craftsman's pleasure the exercise gave to him.

Long before he reached any place of official leadership he had become an untitled leader in the Senate because he gave no overt sign of wishing to be one and because of the rare quality of the advice he gave to his colleagues. Many came to his office and the relationship was on the whole coolly impersonal and much like that of a senior student calling upon his professor for a required conference about his work or future.

Other powerful Senators have told me frankly, if in an understandably private way, "Bob could give you a sense of *security*." There grew up about him a belief not only that his suggestions were honest—which was a fact—but that almost invariably they were sound.

This latter view, while of extremely doubtful validity, probably was brought about most of all by three interrelated circumstances. In the first place, Taft never lacked for an answer of some sort. In the second place his political courage was contagious. In the third place he all but required confidence in his judgment by the manner in which he gave his counsel.

He would not, for example, willingly discuss a fellow Senator's problems if that Senator brought to him only opinions. He would give no advice until he had what he believed to be all the relevant facts in the case, so far as these could be ascertained, and a man making a report to him was let down very hard if his legwork had been inadequate.

Moreover, he was careful not to offer a merely optimistic prognosis of a fellow Senator's doubts and sufferings. Every man has perhaps had the experience of going to one friend when he wanted only to be reassured and to quite a different friend when he wanted a surgical survey of his difficulties. Taft was the surgeon type.

At times, he was rough with the patient. And men calling upon him to *volunteer* their advice to him as the Republican Senate leader were well advised to have a cogent story in hand. He could be brusque to the point of rudeness with the vague or unsuitable. A Republican Senator of some distinction thus describes Taft in this attitude. "When I was in business and a subordinate came to me with an idea that looked pretty dim to me I would say to him, 'Jim, think it

over for a few days and then come to see me again.' That
saved Jim's face, for he probably would consult others then
and they would tell him, or he would find out for himself,
that his idea wasn't so good.

"But Bob worked it the other way. When I went to him
with an idea that he didn't like he would look at me a
minute and then say, 'Why, that's nonsense . . . nonsense.'
You felt sort of foolish, you know. He didn't *mean* to be
nasty; he just liked to get rid of any proposal at once when
he thought it was no good. You would not go back soon,
but you *would* go back when you were sure you really had a
good idea."

But while Taft rarely sought the advice of another, and
never unless he had with that other person some specific
project in motion, his rare approaches for consultation
showed that the doctor could be a patient as well. He had
a curious deference when he called upon another Senator in
those circumstances; he was self-deprecatory and unchar-
acteristically tentative in his views.

The frequency or infrequency of his dealings as the head
of the hierarchy with other Republican Senators had no
necessary relationship to them as individuals or to the degree
of fondness or lack of it that he felt variously toward them.
When he met a Senator frequently it was only because that
Senator at the moment was occupied with something in
which Taft had great interest. *Issues* determined his Senate
associations; personalities were all but irrelevant.

Indeed, fundamentally Taft wanted intelligence simply
in the way and more or less on the terms that an intelligence

officer wants it. While he was so typical of some of the big things in the Senate, he was anything but typical in others. There was no touch of the prima donna in him. Most of his more eminent colleagues were, however, deeply dyed with the artistic temperament, and Taft found this all a great nuisance.

Sometimes in his search for the facts about the status of a certain bill in which the Republicans were involved he would decline to follow the proper channels and would telephone a committee staff member or a Senator's secretary instead of the Senator himself. He called the man he thought knew the most about the matter in which he was concerned at that moment. If wounded Senatorial pride brought repercussions he would not directly acknowledge or dignify the incident. But, if he could remember it long enough, he would try to find an occasion to make an obliquely friendly approach to the offended Senator. He would not, of course, go quite so far as to mention what lay between them.

He was allowed to take many liberties of this kind because he was an enormously skilled legislative technician and, like a gifted man in any office, was permitted to diverge a bit from the norm so long as he delivered the goods.

Deliver them he did, fundamentally because he worked far harder than most Senators, knew far more than most about almost everything except in the field of foreign affairs, and because most of the time he had a luminous candor of purpose that was extraordinarily refreshing in a chamber not altogether devoted to candor.

Then, there was of course the fact that his influence was

not altogether gained by sheer personal qualities. A man who to millions of hard-core Republicans was the greatest man in the United States had to be carefully reckoned with by all who were interested only in the simple equations of naked political power. To fall out openly with Taft was not an undertaking upon which to enter lightly.

Thus it was that a Taft who could be so wrong, and in so diffused a way, on world affairs could continue to draw to himself on domestic affairs so many who so totally disagreed otherwise with him.

The reasoning of his followers—whether all the time or most of the time or some of the time followers—had in it this element: To most any man in the Senate there is no higher political career, barring the White House. And the White House is plainly never going to be open at best at any one time to more than one of the ninety-six members of that distinguished body. So long as one was to stay in the Senate as a Republican what could he lose by association with Taft in the field where Taft was supreme, that is, on domestic matters? In this field there was nowhere else much to go, for rightly or wrongly the non-Taftian Republicans had little practical domestic legislative significance during all his Senate life.

And finally, one must go back, as always, to Taft's personal qualities.

He was, so far as I know, the only elevated Western politician, apart from Churchill, who never used a ghost writer or any of the other aids and trappings of the age of radio and television and of general clamor in the night. He did his speeches the direct way and though they were never brilliant they were at all events his own.

For a major speech "outside"—that is, away from the Senate—that required, say, thirty minutes to deliver he would dictate to a stenographer for about forty-five minutes. He took her typed copy, made a few marks here and there with a pencil, had her type the thing over again, and that was that. Most of the time in speaking in the Senate he had no manuscript of any sort or even notes.

In this, as in larger ways, he had no small instinct of self-protection and his very nearly consistent refusal to buttress himself with a manuscript or to appeal later to the record from misquotations or misinterpretation was, to other politicians, an extraordinarily brave thing. Constantly, he was being misunderstood or only partly understood, sometimes because he usually had an elliptical manner of speaking and could never quit assuming that everybody was going to understand him, and sometimes because, in plain fact, he was not subject to absolute understanding.

When misunderstandings arose he only shook his head, with a sad impatience if the misunderstanding arose in the mind and utterances of a friend or angrily if in the utterance of another. But then he plowed on. He had no real time for anger; he could rage but the storm was usually over within five minutes. Once over, it was really over. He dismissed it all.

For he had no gift for emotion. Much of his solace in life lay in what his bulging brief case contained—many quite fascinating problems, many very sound data.

17

THE NEW ALLIANCE

The inauguration in January, 1953, of General Eisenhower as the first Republican President in the twenty years since Herbert Hoover had gloomily left the White House was not Eisenhower's triumph alone. The President stood, of course, at the center of the stage, but highly prominent in the wings was the tired figure of Robert A. Taft. He was still unalterably ungainly but the long pressure of family and friends had at last succeeded to the extent that it could now be said that his suits no longer looked as though they had been slept in. They still looked as though they had been made for an absent-minded man, but now at least for Taft and not for a much smaller man. Still, the most passionate Taft apologist could not have called him a fashionable dresser and it is a great pleasure to report that this remained the case to the end.

The relationship between these two, Taft as the vanquished "old pro" of the professional section of the Republican party and President Eisenhower as the victorious amateur in the political art, was by this time correct but notably lacking in warmth. It might be said that a small part of Taft's complicated feeling toward President Eisenhower was about what Lord Alexander as an old combat officer must at one time have felt of General Eisenhower as his superior in the war: That fortune had an odd way of promoting to high command those whose combat experience had been notably brief.

And then even by Inauguration Day there had been a number of unfortunate though not frontal collisions between Taft and General Eisenhower, or Eisenhower's closest advisers. Taft felt, with what on objective observation seemed to be considerable justice, that the Eisenhower people had put a remarkably legalistic interpretation upon that aspect of the recent Eisenhower-Taft compact of Morningside Heights in which the new President had engaged not to "discriminate" against Taft men when it came to filling out the places in the new Republican Administration.

While it could not be stated flatly that there had been such "discrimination," a skilled advocate could have made out a fairly good circumstantial case. It was a known fact that not one of the original Taft recommendations for Cabinet posts had been accepted by the President. And in two instances there had been what Taft thought to be extremely pointed and gratuitous thrusts against him.

While even then he admired, and came greatly to admire, George M. Humphrey of Ohio, President Eisenhower's designee for Secretary of the Treasury, Taft nevertheless felt aggrieved at this selection. It turned out that Humphrey, as a citizen of Taft's own state of Ohio, had been chosen without any sort of consultation with Taft himself.

This, in the Senate tradition of which Taft was always a faithful disciple, was a most grievous business. It is customary at least to inform a powerful Senator when one of his constituents is about to be elevated to high place. It is absolutely obligatory to do this when the Senator involved is the Senate leader of the Administration in power and is thus a part of the high command. Moreover, Humphrey, as Taft once told me, had been in the past a good, solid Taft man but in 1952 had allowed himself to go over to the Eisenhower people.

And then, almost simultaneous to the blow delivered to Taft over Humphrey, there came the unkindest cut, the choice of Martin Durkin of the plumbers' union to be Secretary of Labor and thus to sit in a kind of judgment seat over Taft's beloved Taft-Hartley labor act. Durkin was not only a Democrat, which in Taft's view was quite enough wholly to disqualify him, but had vehemently supported the Democratic Presidential nominee, Adlai E. Stevenson. And, worst of all, he had naturally been connected with the long attack of the labor leaders on Taft-Hartley.

Thus, when Durkin's name turned up, Taft was no longer able to sustain the angrily brooding public silence that he found barely possible to maintain in the Humphrey affair. After much thought (this was not one of those sudden spurts of anger that sometimes led him to extreme statement that he later regretted) he issued an edict denouncing the Durkin appointment as an "incredible" one.

He used the adjective not simply as a handy general epithet but in its most precise meaning. He thought the choice of Durkin was indeed incredible, in the sense of unbelievable. It seemed obvious to him that this entry of the famous plumber into what was otherwise called "the Cabinet of millionaires" was not only a conscious slight to Taft but, and much worse, was so incongruous as to be absurd.

He turned out, by the way, to have been at least partly right, for Durkin left the Cabinet within nine months, accusing President Eisenhower of bad faith over certain proposed changes in the Taft-Hartley Act and creating for the Administration a crisis in its labor relations that in all probability could have been avoided by a different approach to the labor post at the outset.

Taft's view of the case was that Durkin was essentially, and had to be, a partisan over the Taft-Hartley Act, a quite honorable attitude in a labor leader but not one well recommending a man to be the Secretary of Labor in the Administration of a President who at Morningside had agreed with Taft that the act was basically a good thing. To be blunt about it, Taft thought the whole episode was altogether too suggestive of an effort to fool the American public into supposing that appeasement of labor leaders was possible and desirable.

And in his simple partisan way he felt that the Democrats had been well and soundly thrashed. Let them take their lumps; lay on, Macduff—all this was his spirit. He simply did not grasp that President Eisenhower, who in his past career had more than once found it possible to compromise the seemingly irreconcilable, could genuinely believe that there could be no harm in attempting, at least, a rapprochement with the labor leaders.

Moreover, Taft was firmly of the opinion that the Durkin

affair was an excessively clear instance of what he considered to be the continued hostility of "the Dewey people" toward him. For as he had not blamed General Eisenhower for the wounding things said about Taft men at the 1952 convention, Taft now exculpated the President personally from knowing complicity in the Durkin episode.

All these things, however, certainly had not done anything to promote the alliance of necessity that Eisenhower as a new Republican President and Taft as an old Republican indispensable were now trying, if in a gingerly way, to raise up. The resulting chill in the atmosphere was, once again, widely misunderstood because of the wide and persistent misunderstanding of Robert A. Taft. There were many predictions that an Eisenhower-Taft break must now soon arrive. Some reached the conclusion as they looked simply as objective forecasters in search of coming events. Others plainly looked as men with pro-Democratic motives; such a rupture would of course have enormously promoted the Democratic fortunes.

This view of *inevitable* quarreling on a high level was perfectly logical but far from sound, Taft being Taft. As one has attempted heretofore to suggest, Taft could get quite angry, but never for long and almost never when the contention involved mere personalities. Only *issues* could deeply move him for long or permit him long to sustain a position of belligerence.

Had the time been reached when issues mortally separated him from President Eisenhower there *would* perhaps have been an explosion, but only if the subject matter was so grave in Taft's view as to justify him in taking a step he never took in all his life—that is, a step to break up a Republican enterprise.

His early attitude toward Durkin, and to a lesser degree toward Humphrey, was only this: It was all extremely annoying to him, much as were other irrational and not soundly Republican manifestations upon which of late his eyes had been forced to rest.

Nevertheless, none of this untidy business engaged his fundamental principles and, apart from this, he was by this time taking a very great interest in foreign affairs and in its approach to this field the new Administration was substantially pleasing him. The extraordinary extent of this foreign interest can be quickly illustrated by the single fact that Taft, when the new Republican Congress opened some two weeks before General Eisenhower took the Presidential oath, had put himself on the Senate Foreign Relations Committee.

To do this he had to leave a senior place on the Finance Committee, which both in terms of its field of jurisdiction and in terms of its profoundly conservative personnel he loved more than any other.

He went on the Foreign Relations Committee in the spirit of a man who is leaving what he likes for what he has always disliked; in a spirit of responding to the grim call of duty. He regarded the Republican chairman of Foreign Relations, Senator Alexander Wiley of Wisconsin, as far from "safe." He once told me as much. He had, of course, nothing to suggest against Wiley's integrity or motives; nevertheless he thought the chairman was by any standard far too pliably internationalist, and becoming more so all the time. "We have got to get a little stronger *conservative* voice on that committee," Taft observed.

And in the meantime, the President, in Taft's view, had himself acted in an adequately conservative way in choosing John Foster Dulles as his Secretary of State. Though Taft and Dulles had not seen many things quite alike in the brief past period of Dulles' membership in the Senate from New York, they were personally sympathetic. This was so, in spite of Dulles' old association with Dewey of New York, because Taft felt Dulles had largely purged himself of this association.

Too, Dulles had at one time held an isolationist view, though this was before Pearl Harbor, and perhaps Taft thought that there was always a faint hope for a Dulles return to the past. At any rate, Taft believed the Dulles appointment to be a good one, no doubt in part because at the 1952 convention the new Secretary of State had kept in touch with the Taft camp quite as much as with the Eisenhower camp and had shown, in Taft's opinion, a genuine desire to see the *Republicans* win. And some of Dulles' earliest actions as Secretary of State greatly pleased the Taft Senate Republicans, if not Taft personally. He accepted a degree of Senatorial intervention in interdepartmental affairs that brought him under much private criticism from liberal Republicans.

Therefore when, early in 1953, Taft began to lead each week to the White House a deputation of Congressional leaders for a legislative conference, this was about the position:

He was far from happy at the Durkin and Humphrey appointments, though in the case of Humphrey he never doubted the essential soundness of the choice but only its untraditional *method*. He thought "the Dewey people," through Attorney General Herbert Brownell, were still conducting at least a limited anti-Taft offensive within the Administration. The fact that he had at no time blamed the President himself for any of this, however, was a most important consideration in his general attitude.

And he felt that the Eisenhower Administration was getting close to the right track on foreign affairs.

He felt, both in the personal and in the ideological sense, a tremendous responsibility to all those Taft people whom, after Morningside, he had advised to go all-out for General Eisenhower. His attitude toward what he considered to be the hard forays of the Dewey wing in the field of patronage was never one of great outrage nor was it ever a feeling of hopelessness.

Just as it was Taft who arranged that President Eisenhower should see the Congressional Republican leaders regularly, it was Taft who prepared, early on, a *modus vivendi* on patronage by which the Administration accepted in principle at least the classic Senate position that if a Senator's recommendations for appointments were to be rejected, this ought at least to be done in the gentlest possible way. This arrangement did not work too well but it was generally satisfactory to Taft. Again, his interest was more in the forms and in the institution of patronage than in the persons or even in the individual jobs involved.

At this period, that is, in early 1953, Taft's visits to the White House were neither glad nor eager; he was slow in thawing out. The White House staff, skillfully advised in this by the President's press officer, James Hagerty, developed quickly, however, a good sense of what might be called Taft Relations as a form of public relations. Though the President's staff associates had had little opportunity to know Taft, beyond the fact that he had called several times at Eisenhower headquarters in New York between election day and inauguration day, they were remarkably perceptive in grasping so well as they did the essential significance of Taft.

They understood his feelings fairly well and they went out of their way to suggest to him that all the hard things said in the past should now be forgotten. From the immediately post-Morningside position of honoring Taft in a general way they now progressed to a firm policy of covering him with quite sincere flattery in specific ways. It is obvious that as they got to know him better they came genuinely to admire him—not in everything, of course, but in his fundamental character. His lack of smallness, for example, was illustrated in his attitude toward Hagerty.

Taft knew, of course, that Hagerty, as an old Dewey associate, had helped to sharpen many an anti-Taft weapon, but he did not, so to speak, visit upon the sons the sins of the fathers. He was entirely friendly with Hagerty, as was entirely natural. For the Taft who took all the blame for the actions of his campaign subordinates was entirely ready to forgive the fairly junior subordinates of his old foeman Dewey. He only thought of Hagerty as having done with proper loyalty what he was assigned to do.

The new entree to the White House, which for two decades had been to him a forbidding and practically an unknown land, itself began to mellow Taft a bit, in spite of himself. And having lived there as a boy he was not easy to impress.

Hagerty saw to it, for example, that Taft spoke to the press, after his meetings with President Eisenhower, not in the noncommittal and informal quasi-public corridors of the executive offices, as did most other visitors, but in Hagerty's own private office. Though this was a subtle thing, and in no measurable way a very important one, it nevertheless had the effect rather of setting Taft apart and above everybody save the President's own highest official family.

And in the meantime the Senator was gathering fresh honors in Congress. He decided to announce that he would be "available" for the post of Senate Republican leader, a place he had for years held in fact while others held it in form. This meant that he must leave the chairmanship of the collective organ of the Republican leadership, the Senate Republican Policy Committee. This leave-taking did not distress him. Laconically he remarked to a friend: "When our party controls the White House most of the Republican policy is made there anyhow."

In spite of it all he actually did not gladly contemplate taking the post of floor leader, because it would leave him less than a suitable amount of time to think, but he determined to make the sacrifice for practical reasons. "You can't have a lot of fellows running down to the White House and then coming back to the Senate to speak for the President," he said. "That voice has got to be one voice."

And since it had to be one voice it had, in Taft's view, to be his voice. This seemed to him wholly obvious, as indeed it was. Though never a man of conceit, except in the area of cerebration, he was never a falsely modest man. When he said he thought he *ought* to take the leadership he meant only that. He was, of course, duly and quickly elected.

He wanted to be *the* Congressional man dealing regularly with President Eisenhower for a variety of reasons. Prominent among these reasons were his continued distrust of "the Dewey people," his sense of special obligation to all the old Taft people all over the country and his simple awareness of the fact that he was perhaps the ablest and certainly the most powerful, and therefore the most responsible, Republican in Congress.

And in spite of the fact that he had been greatly displeased with the Durkin-Humphrey appointments, one of the first tests of his new Senate leadership found him greatly displeased that these and all other Cabinet appointees could not be confirmed by the Senate, according to plan, on inauguration day. Senator Wayne Morse of Oregon, who had left the Republican party during the campaign to come out for Stevenson for President, took advantage of his parliamentary right to block such immediate confirmation. Morse had been lately ostracized by the Republicans for his act of rebellion and shorn of his important committee assignments. Taft did not initiate this disciplinary action; indeed, he regretted it, though not to the extent of trying to call a halt to it. But just as he never seemed too interested in developing new Republicans out of Democrats, he always had the greatest concern to rehabilitate and reclaim all erring *old* Republicans. Finally, he gloomily foresaw that the Republicans would have a good deal of trouble with Morse the expatriate and this seemed to him altogether too bad, especially since he thought it bad tactics for the Republicans to add to Morse's hair shirt.

And, worst of all, the whole business was to Taft somewhat disorderly. The incident of the delayed confirmation had no genuine importance. Still, it annoyed Taft, for President Eisenhower by this time was going to great lengths to state on all possible occasions the enormous value of Congress. Taft was thus anixous to show that he, too, could be magnanimous and get things done for the Administration.

This attitude, a willingness to be magnanimous though not yet a final real acceptance of Eisenhower as President, typified the early phase of the official association of Taft the Republican leader and President Eisenhower in the White House.

18

TO MAKE THE
ADMINISTRATION *WORK*

The second and final phase of Robert A. Taft's relationship with President Eisenhower was surely one of the most curious ever devised by men. For the first few weeks Taft was carefully noncommittal, even to friends, as to what personal view he took of the President. And then, in March, he returned to the Capitol from the White House one day to observe to an intimate: "*He* [President Eisenhower] is, I think, a man of good will."

A few weeks later, again after a consultation with the President, Taft now observed: "*He* is grasping things pretty well; I find that he remembers all the substance of a conversation we had about two months ago and the proposals I made to *him* then."

This did not mean that all was entirely serene. More than once Taft came back to the Senate in imperfectly concealed disgust with what he had, or had not, heard at the White House. He said on one occasion, when the subject had been budgets and taxes, "*They* don't know *what* they want. Until they do know, there is surely not much that I can do."

His attitude then was that the President was *trying* but that there was a vast amount of educational work that had, regrettably, to be done before he could be presumed to be abreast of matters that to Taft were quite plain and routine.

The Senator made on the whole a great effort to keep these thoughts to himself. Since Morningside Heights his one basic determination had been to make this Republican Administration work; for he feared that if in any capital way it failed nearly all Republicans would be the sufferers for many years to come.

The exceeding thinness of the Republican Congressional victory in the 1952 elections, which was, of course, desperately meager in contrast to the personal victory achieved by General Eisenhower at the head of the Republican ticket, had caused Taft great concern and he did not for a moment forget its implications. It was his somewhat illogical view that General Eisenhower's far better showing was to a great extent attributable to the heavy Taft intervention in his behalf but that the position of the predominantly Taft Republican party in Congress, which was always his highest interest, was far too insecure.

He began, therefore, a characteristic campaign to improve this position—by making that Congress more Taftian than ever. At the White House he slowly and powerfully urged upon President Eisenhower the adoption of what was basically a Taft Republican view of domestic political issues. It is obvious, though not of course a matter actually of record, that he pressed upon the President his own institutional view of the Republican party.

There were, for example, many who thought that the President's somewhat mixed public attitude toward Senator

Joseph R. McCarthy, whom he was privately represented to detest, was an example of Taft's work. For Taft looked upon McCarthy simply as a powerful and important Republican, who would be greatly useful in the 1954 Congressional campaigns as he had been in others, and thus as a man entitled at least to the benevolent neutrality of the White House, if not its actual shelter. At all events it came about that the President seemed alternately to strike out at what is called McCarthyism and to decline to offer any criticism of the author of McCarthyism.

Speaking generally, that part of the President's McCarthy policy that was clearly hostile was representative of the feelings of the President himself and of the Dewey and/or Eisenhower Republicans alike. But his refusal to engage McCarthy directly or in any clear way was representative of the practically unanimous advice of the Taft Republicans.

It thus developed, in the second phase of the Eisenhower-Taft relationship, that the Dewey Republicans could claim the greater second-level influence within the Administration's official Cabinet structure but Taft could claim the greater influence over the whole ideology of the Administration.

The clouds that in the special Congressional elections of late 1953 began to gather over Republican prospects for continued control of Congress in 1954 thus were more fairly attributable to Taft than to the Dewey people. Not only had he alone dominated the Congress that now seemed to be in some early disfavor; he had, in the legislative sense at least, dominated the Eisenhower Administration's philosophy.

The White House meetings between Taft and President Eisenhower meantime well illustrated the great differences in personality between these two. The President often addressed Taft as "Bob," and never more formally than "Senator," which when used without the surname is in Washington life a greeting both of informality and of friendliness.

Taft on his side was never heard at the White House, even in the warmth of face-to-face general legislative and political discussions with Eisenhower, to use any salutation less formal than "Mr. President." Once in a while, away from the atmosphere of the White House, he would privately and to a friend refer to "Ike," but even in making informal reports to correspondents at the Capitol about this or that meeting with Eisenhower the Senator always referred only to "The President."

Though he was thus never able really to unbend—not even on a golf course with the President, according to the most authoritative information—Taft responded warmly, inside himself, to the President's relaxed and amiable manner. He even liked the "Bob," though few had the hardihood to use that nickname. Like many shy and distant men, he could be charmed by an informality that he himself could rarely achieve.

But none of this could sweeten the tartness of the Taft tongue or soften its superb tactlessness. Once at the White House, when the topic of conversation was the appointment of a man to head the Veterans Administration, one of those on the White House side of the table suggested the name of a certain general. "No, no!" Taft snapped, looking

directly at a man named Eisenhower who had been something of a general himself. "No more generals! No more
generals!"

The Senator, in telling this story later to members of his
family, complained ruefully: "And the trouble was that
nobody even laughed."

Mrs. Oveta Culp Hobby of Texas, President Eisenhower's
Secretary of Health, Education and Welfare, collided with
a somewhat similar Taft prejudice that caused her newly
created department to get its long and dissonant name and
no doubt to be forever under the threat of being called
"HEW." When she went to the new Republican Congress
in 1953 in support of the Administration's bill to elevate to
Cabinet status what had been the old Federal Security
Agency, she proposed that it be called Department of the
General Welfare. In this she was guided by a more than
adequate traditionalism in the best Taft definition. She got
her proposed title out of the Constitution of the United
States, which in its preamble of course uses the phrase
". . . promote the general welfare."

Mrs. Hobby found that not even so Midwestern a Republican as Representative Clare Hoffman of Michigan, who
was in charge of the bill on the House side, had any objection to her attempt at nomenclature. And Hoffman is a
famous terror to the bureaucrats.

But then Taft came upon the scene on the Senate side.
"That's just what I'm trying to get away from," he protested
to Mrs. Hobby. One of his favorite gibes against the Truman Administration had been that it had sought a "welfare

state." Therefore, there could now be no talk of welfare alone. Mrs. Hobby quickly agreed to drop "general welfare." The little incident is not a bad illustration of the degree of the Administration's anxiety not to offend Taft, nor of his power.

Since he felt ultimately responsible for legislation, he had no hesitation in vetoing Administration nomenclature (or legislative projects if it came to that). He was returning to that attitude of personal responsibility that he had so well maintained in the old Republican Eightieth Congress, had so regrettably abandoned for a time after a repudiation of that Congress, and had for the most part taken up again in his race for re-election from Ohio in 1950.

On the other hand, he naturally pursued the orthodox policy of rendering unto Caesar. He was greatly jealous of the prerogatives of Congress but he would not permit other Republicans to intrude too far upon the White House— though his notion of what was an intrusion was kind to the Congressional definition of that term.

He took up generally, however, what can only be called a protective attitude toward the President and the White House. When he thought the President was wrong or ill-advised he went to him and said so, but once the White House was deeply committed, Taft's strong impulse was to accommodate himself to the situation. In consequence he swallowed a good many things that were not palatable to him, but nothing directly challenging any of his basic principles.

He began to look upon President Eisenhower much as a

Labour Minister in the British Government might look upon
the Crown—that is, that the Presidency (with a Republican
incumbent) was an indispensable institution and that who-
ever held it was entitled to full co-operation to the last
possible point consistent with fundamental convictions. Or,
as Walter Lippmann once put it, Taft began to act as a kind
of Prime Minister for the President. The President, in this
view of the case, had something of the status of a Constitutional monarch or a Head of State in the French sense.

This is not to suggest that Taft did not develop personal
respect and even affection for President Eisenhower, for to
a point he did. He was simply aware that the President was
a newcomer in the most difficult old profession of politics
and he felt entirely competent to give a decisive form of
advice when it came to all questions of faithfully representing both the point of view and the political necessities of
the orthodox Republicans.

What the President's responding personal attitude may
have been is subject only to speculation. A reasonably informed guess is that he entirely understood Senator Taft's
great value to his Administration, not simply because of
Taft's position in Congress but because of the large part of
the Republican party that so faithfully he typified and led.
The President was not unacquainted with both the necessity
and the desirability of closing up against an enemy force
by making alliances that need not in all respects be entirely
comfortable but were nevertheless extremely useful.

And he had known, moreover, how to put together the
advice of various men into a pattern that ultimately became

an Eisenhower decision. If the pattern in this case was heavily colored with Taft, it was nevertheless President Eisenhower's pattern at the end. Perhaps this is how the President approached Taft; in any case the approach was a successful one.

For Taft's function in this period was not only to check and veto the Administration, but powerfully to promote it, and in many ways. No other man could have so quieted the anti-Eisenhower feeling of the Republican traditionalists in Congress; Taft was their only leader. No other man could have forced a general acceptance of the President in the Republican Congress, however reluctant this acceptance was in many instances.

And no other man could at the same time have moved so surely to cut to the absolute minimum the latent and prospective influence of the very men, such as Senators Duff of Pennsylvania and Saltonstall of Massachusetts, who had done so much back in the days when the undertaking had not looked too hopeful to make Eisenhower President of the United States.

It might have been thought ordinarily that the men who had created the boom for Eisenhower would sit very high among the mighty when he ascended to the White House. Not a bit of it. Duff, Saltonstall and all the other leading original-Eisenhower Senators were smoothly thrust by Taft into far-back seats. It became a commonplace in Washington to suggest, with some truth, that the surest way to Eisenhower's favor in Congress was to have been a pro-Taft and an anti-Eisenhower man before the 1952 convention.

Taft accomplished the isolation in the Senate of the Duffs with techniques and for reasons that will by now be familiar. In the first place, they had as a group little Senate seniority and thus their shield was not strong. In the second place, the Senate being the Senate, the fact that they had been associated at the very outset with a successful President-making did not necessarily endear them there. In the third place, the Taft people everywhere held the critical points of Senate control. They held the bulk of the Senate legislative committee chairmanships. They held all the ultimate places of party power. For example, in 1953 the Senate Republican Policy Committee, which is the whole Senate hierarchy, had eleven seats, of which precisely one was occupied by an early and ardent Eisenhower backer, Senator Saltonstall.

And finally, the White House itself came in no visible way to the succor of the beleagured group of its original partisans in the Senate. Duff, one of the most advanced and one of the ablest, was allowed to wander about rather lonely. Saltonstall's nature was not in any event such as to permit him to contend for privilege.

The reality of the situation simply was this. While the Taft Republicans had again shown in their preconvention struggles with the Eisenhower forces that they could not win the national prize, they were if anything stronger than ever in Congress. For the unwillingness or inability—and inability probably more nearly fits the case—of the Eisenhower White House to give aid and comfort to its first and and most faithful Congressional followers was a lesson not lost upon all concerned. Taft, for his part, was never unable to help or in one way or another to punish.

To the small extent that he ever turned to others, Taft unusually turned again, of course, to the old Taft people in the Senate when there were small or large prizes to be had or small or large recognitions to be granted. And he himself stood very largely and grandly in the whole field of national decisions and national actions.

In one sense the President had to deal with him substantially as a co-equal, or as one Power dealing with an Allied Power that is very nearly as strong. And Taft while accepting the perquisites that went with this odd position of affairs was faithful to the commitments that it implied.

No President within twenty years—that is, neither Roosevelt nor Truman—had so effective a Senate leader as Eisenhower had in Taft in the brief months between the Republican return to power in January of 1953 and Taft's death in July. This might not have been so had either Mr. Roosevelt or Mr. Truman been willing to listen to his Senate spokesman with the rare attention that President Eisenhower gave to Taft. And Taft usually carried forward programs which were more or less negotiated; the Democratic leaders before him had had to try to carry forward programs in which they were on the whole little consulted until after the critical decisions had been made.

Nevertheless, the fact of the business was that in the field of power politics President Eisenhower had found in Taft an instrument of incomparable and unique usefulness— unique because in the Senator the President could draw upon the very qualities that he himself did not have and could by no imagining soon develop.

Taft proved in this period a suspicion long held by political writers, and it was this: that while he was always quick to cheer on as statesmanship all rebellions within the Democratic party he had not the slightest intention of allowing these irregularities to rise in any marked way when *his* party was in power.

He proved also that there is usually in all Republican enterprises at least an outward seeming of order and unity that is usually absent in all Democratic enterprises. Whether he proved as well that the suppression of these internal disorders is good for a party in the long run may be determined in part when the Congressional elections of 1954 have come and gone.

The association of President Eisenhower and Senator Taft displayed on the President's part a spirit of generosity in allowing the emergence of one who almost was his rival for power and on Taft's part a magnificent loyalty to an *idea* of Republicanism. But it was not an intellectually tenable association. Though it was a practically sound association for the short course, since it saved the Eisenhower Administration at the outset from much trouble and travail, it rested on the fact that too much had been brushed under the rug to achieve this unity.

The Eastern internationalist Republicans in the 1952 convention had had it in their power to come to grips in a definite way with all that Taft embodied. They chose instead to take the opportunity given by the Taft people themselves to defeat him by what actually was almost an irrelevancy—the clamor about "stolen delegates"—when the issues really rested on a great contest between two whole sets of national and world views. For a healthy Republican party one set or the other set must at length prevail, and prevail clearly and away from the shadow of mere collateral contentions.

Another time there will be no guarantee of the final unselfishness of another Taft or of the negotiating skill of another Eisenhower.

19

CLEAN BILL FOR BOHLEN

The most significant single service done by Taft for President Eisenhower was, stated in a bald and simple way, to lead the Senate on March 27, 1953, to confirm by a vote of 74 to 13 the President's nomination of Charles E. Bohlen to be Ambassador to Moscow. Vastly more than Bohlen and than the Moscow mission, for all its extremely delicate function in the cold war, was in fact involved.

And there was more even than the maintenance of the general prestige of a newly elected President, which is a matter of the highest importance, indeed. For at issue here were the most fundamental things: Would the Eisenhower Administration, which had been fewer than four months in office, be able to conduct even the mere housekeeping aspects of its foreign policy without harsh and endless Senate interference? Would the Cabinet position of Secretary of State John Foster Dulles, so recently established in high office, remain a tenable position? The question was real and acute, for though the President personally had selected Bohlen, Dulles had put his whole power back of that selection.

Bohlen, a career foreign service officer and himself a Republican, had been at the Yalta Conference in 1945, at which Franklin D. Roosevelt for the United States and Winston Churchill for Britain had made their interminably debated concessions to Stalin in order to get him to go into the war against Japan.

These concessions amounted to an agreement by President Roosevelt and Prime Minister Churchill to let the Russians hold formerly Polish territory, which they already held, and Dairen and Port Arthur. It could not be seriously denied that this was a great blow to the tragic Poles, upon whom seemed always to fall the evilest of all the war's evil consequences, and that it much clouded the future for the Chinese Nationalists.

At all events, Yalta to the orthodox Republicans, and to some not so orthodox, had become an undying political issue and a place of infamy. For years they had charged that Yalta had been a "betrayal" of the Poles and of the Chinese Nationalists. Indeed, it was this odd place name in the Crimea that was geographically the base of a clamor that rose to a crescendo in the 1952 Presidential election in the general Republican accusation that both during and after the Second World War the Democrats had been ready to "sell out" free peoples to promote the interests of the Soviet Union.

Bohlen, one of the few Western experts in the Russian language and presumably in understanding of the ways of the Kremlin, had served officially at Yalta as an interpreter, though the Republican line has been that he was in fact a good deal more than that.

The 1952 Republican foreign policy platform, which

Dulles himself had largely constructed in his efforts to find
a plank upon which either General Eisenhower or Senator
Taft could reasonably stand, had called in substance for a
repudiation of the Yalta decisions—decisions so long in con-
troversy afterward that old Senator Tom Connally of Texas,
the Democratic foreign policy leader in his day, once told
a friend from the depths of his exasperation and weariness,
"Oh, God, Yalta this and Yalta that!"

Nevertheless, President Eisenhower sent Bohlen's name
forward to the Senate in February of 1953 to be our Ambassador to Russia. Summoned before the Senate Foreign Relations Committee, which had the duty to make preliminary
inquiry as to whether he ought or ought not be confirmed,
Bohlen declined to take the easy way. He refused to join
in the condemnation of Yalta so long made. He defended
the arrangements there as in the best interests of the United
States at the time they were made though he conceded that
they might appear questionable in the aftertime, in light of
the persistent violation by the Russians of the undertakings
they had entered there.

In spite of this extraordinary attitude, and due in no small
measure to Taft's attitude, Bohlen was at length "cleared"
by the Foreign Relations Committee with its unanimous
vote. Taft and Senator William F. Knowland of California,
who was to succeed him as the Senate Republican leader,
went along ungladly with the nominee. The committee
chairman, Senator Alexander Wiley of Wisconsin, announced that Secretary Dulles had himself "evaluated" a

report by the Federal Bureau of Investigation and had stated that this report left "no doubt of Mr. Bohlen's loyalty and security."

Taft was distinctly unhappy, both with the fact that the President had selected Bohlen when it was indisputably clear that the President had run on a very anti-Yalta platform and with the fact that Senator Wiley had not seen fit early on to have a deputation of Senators themselves review the FBI file. And as Taft had known it would, a passionate clatter arose in the Senate on this point.

Senator McCarthy began to organize a movement to refuse Senate confirmation to Bohlen, first raising suggestions against his "security" and then proceeding to the more general complaint that he had been associated with "the old Acheson gang," meaning the group around Dean Acheson, who had been Mr. Truman's Democratic Secretary of State.

Other orthodox Republicans, prominent among them Senator Styles Bridges of New Hampshire, who was in the sense of seniority the Republican dean of the Senate, advanced to the attack on a simpler ground. They argued that Bohlen could be said to symbolize Yalta, which he had refused to disavow, and that it could thus be said that "the change" so widely promised by the Republicans in the 1952 campaign was not going to be very marked, after all, in this area of affairs at least. And they said that to send Bohlen to Russia would be a most curious proceeding specifically in light of all that Dulles' foreign policy plank had said about Yalta.

Taft was at once and clearly, but only momentarily, thrust into a dilemma. *He* had long abominated Yalta. *He* had been in the forefront of those crying out for repudiation. And *he* had, as a powerful candidate for the 1952 Republican Presidential nomination, gladly accepted the convention's demand for repudiation.

On the other hand there was here plainly a matter of tradition and decorous procedure. Everybody at all familiar with the situation knew quite well that it was so customary as almost to be unwritten law that any new President had a right to pick his associates—and especially his envoys to foreign powers. The Senate's Constitutional function to "advise and consent" was nearly always the merest formality.

Moreover, Taft was aware that in the anti-Bohlen demonstration had appeared a small but menacing cloud over the prospects for Mr. Eisenhower to have an opportunity for an *orderly* Republican Administration. For the Senate to reject Bohlen outright would at any point have been all but unthinkable. But for the Senate to accept him only grudgingly and on a sort of clearly implied probation—a distinct possibility at one time—would have been in the atmosphere of the moment equivalent to a repudiation of a Republican President on his very first test with the Senate.

Taft therefore watched with keen distaste the developing row among the Republicans—the more so because the Democrats, who stood all but unanimously for Bohlen, were grinning in anticipation at this strange embarrassment to the majority. Thus spurred, he had no difficulty in deciding where to put his weight. Contemptuously and publicly he rejected McCarthy's proposal that Dulles be required to testify under oath about the circumstances in which Bohlen had been "cleared" in the State Department for the post. Contemptuously he declined to enter at all the discussion as to whether Dulles himself had given this clearance or whether a security officer, R. W. Scott McLeod, who had been placed in the State Department by right-wing Republicans, had been "overruled."

To Taft's mind the thought of asking a Secretary of State to answer whether or not he had overruled a subordinate was irrelevant and the sheerest of nonsense. It was, of course, his traditional view that Dulles as head of the Department was responsible for all in it, all that it did, and all that it said. And similarly, while he thought the Bohlen appointment most inept, the same sort of reasoning held here. He did not really blame Bohlen for anything that had or had not been done at Yalta, as he did not blame his own people for anything ever done in the name of Taft.

Accordingly, on March 23, Taft arose in the Senate to put an end to what he considered to be a great deal of painful clacking that could have been avoided by a sounder choice for the Moscow appointment. Majestically, he ignored McCarthy's suggestion that Bohlen submit to a "lie detector" test. Then he went on:

"In the first place, the suggestion has been made that Mr. Dulles be called before the Committee on Foreign Relations and be placed under oath. This has hardly been seriously

supported. I think it is a ridiculous suggestion. Mr. Dulles'
statement *not* under oath is just as good as Mr. Dulles'
statement under oath, as far as I am concerned.

"It has now been suggested that the Committee on Foreign Relations call Mr. McLeod. I should be very much
opposed to such a suggestion as that. After all, we have
before us a peculiar kind of question with reference to this
file. Here is a file gathered by the FBI containing every
kind of material with reference to what Mr. X, Mr. Y, or
Mr. Z have said.

"It is a file which never should be published in general circulation. *Just how far it should go among Senators without
becoming a matter of general circulation is a question I
cannot answer.*" This clear suggestion that there *were* Senators who would be prepared to break the confidence of the
file drew no challenge from the floor. Taft stalked out and
for the moment left it at that.

President Eisenhower, for his part, meantime put all his
own influence and that of the White House behind Bohlen,
even to the extent of pointing out that he himself had been
a guest in Bohlen's home.

The right-wing Republican fire went on vigorously, however, and Taft, caught up in one of the most unpleasant
incidents of his life, now agreed to serve with Senator John J.
Sparkman, the Alabama Democrat, on a sort of Senate jury
of two to go to the State Department and look into the FBI
summary of the Bohlen file. This they did on March 24,
1953, and Taft did not relish the experience. He thus dryly
reported, in part, to the Senate on March 25:

"I read the summary through and after doing so I would have asked very strenuously to see the raw files if there were anything in the summary which seemed to be ambiguous or in any way incomplete or which suggested that something which might be in the raw files was omitted; or at least I would have asked to see a portion of the testimony of the informants. But I could not find in the summary anything of that nature. . . .

"So far as I know no suggestion has been made by anyone that there is in the files anything which is not fully covered in the summary. The so-called sixteen pages of derogatory information [much had been made of this, in a general way, by the anti-Bohlenites] relate to entirely separate matters. The greater part of it consists of statements of persons who disagree with Mr. Bohlen's principles with respect to foreign policy.

"They think he played perhaps a larger part than others played in the Yalta conversations and that he was closer to Mr. Acheson than they would like. In other words, they were statements of political differences with Mr. Bohlen.

"So far as I remember there was no one who did not end up by saying that although he disagreed politically, he had full confidence in the morality and the general standing and reputation of Mr. Bohlen.

"There was no suggestion anywhere by anyone reflecting on the loyalty of Mr. Bohlen in any way or any association by him with Communism or support of Communism or even tolerance of Communism.

"When it comes to the question of whether there is any

reason to think that Mr. Bohlen is in any way a security
risk such testimony as there is on that subject relates solely
to the fact that Mr. Bohlen has at times entertained in his
home persons who are considered by the investigators of the
Department as bad security risks.

"I could not find in the summary (of) testimony anything
which seemed to me to raise even a prima facie case or to
support any prima facie evidence that Mr. Bohlen had in
any way ever done anything which would make him a bad
security risk.

"The associations he had were those which anyone might
have had with persons who were friends of many other
people, who may have stayed overnight, or for the week
end, at the home of Mr. and Mrs. Bohlen. But in all the
summary I could see nothing which could create the most
remote guilt-by-association accusation that could be thought
of.

"There was not any suggestion that would in my opinion
create even a prima facie case or a prima facie charge of
any ill-doing on the part of Mr. Bohlen."

This handsome Taftian vindication must surely have been
one of the most impressive scenes, in its way, ever to be
drawn out before the United States Senate. Its impact was
very heavy. The opposition to Bohlen was driven down to
its irreducible core; Taft commanded this position as few
parliamentary men had ever commanded another.

No one dared seriously to question him. Remote, displeased, he put the subject—particularly the ugly hearsay
and rumor that the FBI has always wisely sought to keep

in confidence while appropriate authority concentrates on the evaluation of the facts—away with a motion almost of physical disgust.

But for Taft's towering prestige, his self-sacrifice in swallowing a small *personal* symbol of Yalta (and it will be later seen that this qualification is an important one), President Eisenhower would have fallen onto very hard times in the Bohlen affair. The opposition to Bohlen found itself, because of Taft's decisive intervention, powerless to state its case with any practical coherence. To those who wished to lean upon innuendo against Bohlen, Taft had simply cried "rubbish!" And to suggest that *Taft* had become "soft" on matters of communism or security was too absurd even to attempt.

And to those Republicans who sought—with a good deal of logic, assuming that the Republican platform had really meant what it said—to say that there was an incongruity in now elevating Bohlen, Taft had a wonderfully illogical but politically unanswerable rebuttal: *He* was prepared to consent that Bohlen should go to Moscow, and everybody knew where *he* stood in regard to Yalta.

Nevertheless Taft, having mightily exerted himself to save the Administration from what he considered the strange gaucheness of its selection (and incidentally to save a personal career), passed word to the White House: "No more Bohlens!"

The episode had been good for the Senator, in several ways. To be approved, as he was on this occasion, by so many whose habit had been to denounce him brought him a wry amusement, as had been the case years before when he had stopped the Truman bill to draft the striking railroad men. But while he smiled at these good words from the "internationalists," he was all the same not wholly unimpressed. It had been pleasant to be associated once again with those who in so many personal ways were his natural associates but with whom he was so rarely able to walk in comradeship. And he had not at all minded being in the position to run up, on this issue, a small warning signal to Senator McCarthy that it was still Taft who was directing the Republican party in the Senate.

Still, and characteristically, he did not push matters beyond this point. Asked afterward whether all that had gone on had indicated any split in the Republican party, he replied with impatience and with vehemence: "No, no, no, no!" So far as the Republicans in the Senate were concerned, he wished the episode to be regarded as closed. He was not at all unhappy, however, that the White House had thus learned, so early, that it was most unwise to make delicate appointments in the field of foreign policy, as in any other, without some form of clearance at least with the Taft men, some of whom had left their chief in this instance to oppose Bohlen to the end.

Thus, though his usefulness to President Eisenhower had been enormous and spectacular—a kind of effective service that Eisenhower's predecessor, Harry Truman, had never been able to obtain in any reasonably similar set of circumstances—it had another meaning, too. The other meaning was that Taft was moving forward to consolidate the arrangements made at Morningside. Heretofore, he had stamped his own philosophy over the Administration's approach to many domestic questions. It now was to come about also that the Administration was not again to attempt seriously to move against his wishes on a matter of foreign policy.

"You know," he said to a friend when the Bohlen affair had run its course and had been safely tucked away, "I do not always swallow *everything*."

20

THE "PRIME MINISTER"
AT HIS PEAK

The Taft who helped President Eisenhower to obtain a handsome Senate confirmation of his choice of a pro-Yalta emissary to Moscow, Charles E. Bohlen, was acting with a personal generosity not untouched by a passion for *Republican* order.

This Taft had succeeded within less than a month another Taft—a Taft determined not to let the President dim the favorite old Republican campaign issue, "Yalta." The Senator easily forgave Bohlen; fairly easily he forgave President Eisenhower for making the appointment. But Yalta he never forgave, and President Eisenhower he never allowed to forget that this was so.

On February 2, 1953, the President, in his State of the Union message, had denounced the "enslavement" of free peoples by secret agreements and had declared: "I shall ask the Congress at a later date to join in an appropriate resolution making clear that this Government recognizes no kind of commitment contained in secret understandings of the past which permit this kind of enslavement."

While the Democrats sat looking most uncomfortable, the Republicans of both Houses of Congress, assembled in the

House chamber to hear the address, cheered mightily and with glowing faces. They supposed that the President as one of his first official acts was going to move to repudiate Yalta, though no one suggested very clearly how a declaration by the United States could alter the fact that the Russians now controlled all Poland through satellite Communist organisms and had their friends, at least, in control not simply of part of China but of all the mainland.

It might not be much, so the Republicans reasoned, but at least it was a proper gesture of condemnation of the Democrats and particularly of Franklin Roosevelt's part at Yalta.

There arose for the Administration, however, certain unpleasant realities, the principal one of which was the simple fact that President Eisenhower on foreign policy in no sense controlled the Republican part of Congress, whereas President Eisenhower on foreign policy had the willing support of the vast majority of the Democrats there. The Democrats put the word about that while they would be very unhappy to part with the President on a world issue, since they had long been together on such as these, they would not find it in their hearts to support any manifesto that disparaged Franklin Roosevelt.

Mr. Eisenhower's Secretary of State, Dulles, in the meantime had in mind great projects by which he might at least kindle the *idea* of eventual liberation among the Soviet captive nations and the first step was to be a resolution making clear that the United States considered liberation a realizable, if a distant, goal. He had fixed his heart and hopes on the Yalta resolution. Mr. Eisenhower's people, therefore, confronted a not unprecedented problem in politics as the science of the possible.

They wished to move emotionally at least as far away from Yalta as they could; but while the Republicans would welcome this with high clamors of joy there was the old question of what was feasible in this less than perfect world. To alienate the Democrats, who were in the area of foreign policy far more pro-Eisenhower than all but a handful of Eastern Republicans, was unthinkable. There was moreover the sensitive international question that if Franklin Roosevelt was culpable at Yalta, what was Winston Churchill?

The result of it all, therefore, was about what could have been confidently predicted, given all these circumstances. The President sent up to Congress on February 20 a proposed resolution by which Congress was going to denounce the Russians for having "perverted" the Yalta and associated agreements in order to subjugate free peoples and was going to proclaim that the people of the United States "are never acquiescent in such enslavement." This, and no more.

The effect of this on Taft's orthodox Republicans, and their leader himself, may be quickly indicated simply by saying that the Democrats could hardly conceal their elation at the President's text. There was nothing here that struck at the memory of Mr. Roosevelt—and the fact was that the *Russians* alone were being blamed for the ill things that had followed Yalta.

It would be inaccurate to say that Taft was astonished;

he had, here as elsewhere, a considerable capacity for surprise. Nevertheless, he was most unhappy—and this time in a positive way. While Dulles was entreating the Republicans in Congress to forget many things and approve the Presidential text unaltered, the President himself was observing that it did no good to rake over the dead ashes of the past. Taft and his followers, who considered these ashes to be brightly alight, were coldly unimpressed with the President's reasoning. They set out upon various proposed hardening amendments until Taft moved in to put his approval upon *the* amendment.

This was to be a stipulation that in adopting the resolution Congress was not passing "on the validity or *invalidity*" of Yalta itself. This, of course, was equivalent to saying that Congress held a doubt, at least, that Mr. Roosevelt had the right to enter the undertakings he had entered. The Democrats at once arose in full cry.

They let it be known that they had understood the Eisenhower Administration to have given a commitment that no change in the text would be tolerated. The entire Democratic leadership of the Senate, headed by Senator Lyndon B. Johnson of Texas, met and decided to fight *any* alteration to the end. Taft's own attitude, by this time, was almost equally one of irritation and an objective sense of amusement. He recognized that the Democrats had got the Republicans into a difficult situation, with one small wing of the Republican party ready to go uphill with President Eisenhower and the Taft wing running downhill with Taft. The position appealed to his keen political sense; those who knew him well were reasonably certain that he had a genuine admiration for the hard, quick maneuvering by which Senator Johnson and his Democratic associates had put themselves in domination over this affair.

(And, indeed, the fact is that Taft and Johnson, who was two decades his junior, got along fine most of the time. Johnson, one of the most personable men in the Senate, was a natural member of the club. Taft, though of course deploring the undoubted fact that this young man was a Democrat, nevertheless was inclined to forgive him that because he was, after all, a Southerner. Taft's view was that one must unhappily expect a Southerner to be a Democrat, tradition being what it was, but that any other who took up that party had a good deal to explain.

(Johnson, who has a gift for people in the mass that Taft wholly lacked, had the deepest affection for his Republican opposite number. He was one of the few men who could persistently heckle Taft, as he often did with soft mutters across the three feet of aisle space that separated their desks in the Senate, and not be glared down.)

The proposed manifesto against enslavement had been drawn up in the State Department with what Taft took to have been an entirely inadequate consultation with him and an entirely inadequate regard for the traditional Republican position on the subject of Yalta.

He persisted with his amendment in the full knowledge that the Democrats had vowed to put an end to the whole enterprise before accepting any change and in the knowledge that the Eisenhower Administration was not prepared, at the showdown, to risk a rupture with the Democrats. His motive in this was dual. He was determined not to permit Eisenhower to exculpate Roosevelt, particularly in pursuit of a purpose that he found it impossible to regard as of high importance, and he had a typically Taftian reaction to the language that the Administration had put into the resolution.

He persisted in believing that the Republicans had meant exactly what they said about Yalta in the 1952 platform and in declining to recognize, or in being unable to recognize, that many very important and valuable public men did not put upon campaign promises the absolutely literal meaning that he did.

In short, his attitude here was moored upon a matter of inflexible *principle*; in the case of Bohlen it was to be a case of a *personality*—and in Taft's opinion not too important a personality, at that. Always he had the greatest distaste for anything that seemed to him to be evasive or too "diplomatic," as he thought the Administration's approach to be in this case. And, of course, he was entirely unable to see any reason at all why the President should concern himself in the slightest as to whether the *Democrats* would or would not like what he did about this or anything else.

Plain speaking was to him not simply a habit but almost a fetish. He was, for example, the only really eminent politician known to Washington correspondents who not only never asked them to treat with him in an "off the record" way but actively disliked this method.

Cornered upon a point that he would have preferred not to discuss, he would answer, in a flat, downright way, any sensible question. Perhaps he would now and then look a little wistfully at the interviewer, with an expression that *could* have been taken to mean "I hope you can see your way clear to handling this business with discretion." But he would have wholly disdained making any appeal to that effect. Only tolerating newspapermen in general, he was nevertheless genuinely tolerant of them. A few he liked as individuals; nearly all, however, he rather distrusted. He thought them a regrettably harum-scarum lot and too inclined to be "New Dealers." Sometimes he applied this term in a rather startling way—as it happens to men who actually regarded *him* as in some ways too liberal.

It was this sort of man, with these sorts of attitudes, who ended the Eisenhower Administration's intention to come out against "enslavement." And he did this in no dramatic way, but only by insisting on his reservation in circumstances in which this insistence was fatal to the enterprise. The Democrats remaining adamant, the whole thing simply was allowed quietly to expire and as it fell out Taft never had really to break with the President on the issue.

This curiously subtle and negative little victory was in all his career Taft's only direct and personal victory on a question of foreign policy. But in an allied field in which he had greatly interested himself, that of high military policy, the story was a somewhat different one in the days of his "prime ministership" to President Eisenhower.

Ever since the Senate's Great Debate of 1950–51 on the issue of sending American ground troops to Europe (in which he had set off in a position of violent opposition and had come around eventually to saying that perhaps it was all right to send a few) Taft's view of the United States high command had become sourer and sourer.

It was his opinion that in this debate the then chairman of the Joint Chiefs of Staff, General Omar Bradley, had intervened politically to support the Administration's case and he went so far as publicly to question General Bradley's military integrity. The old Infantry Generals of the George Marshall school already, of course, were in Taft's black books, but the spare, laconic Bradley had got himself unusually in bad—probably because he actually was a good deal like Taft himself and only knew evasion in the sense that it could be found as a word in the dictionary.

And Taft, as it will be remembered, had begun more than a year before the 1952 election to develop a Taftian military concept that ran completely athwart the Bradley concept of "balanced force." Something in these circumstances had to give, and since the Republicans had won the election the identity of this something was instantly clear to Taft.

By April of 1953 Taft was saying, rather softly but insistently, that President Eisenhower should not await in the ordinary way the expiration of the terms of General Bradley and his colleagues on the Joint Chiefs of Staff but should set up at once a new "stand-by" Joint Chiefs organization to undertake, even before its formal succession to power, a review of all military policy. His argument here was that General Bradley and his associates were clearly committed to, and had an intellectual vested interest in the existing policy and that it needed new heads to look in new directions.

The President accepted Taft's philosophy in what probably was the first instance in this country's history where a member of the United States Senate had so casually overturned a whole chain of command. By May the Bradley group was being replaced.

Taft was overjoyed. But having accomplished his purpose he sought no credit. Rather he retired to a position of exaggerated anonymity and pretended, until pressed by friends, that it had all happened in a quite fortuitous way. Still, he could not wholly conceal the way he felt, particularly when an Admiral with strong Asian interests, Arthur Radford, succeeded General Bradley, the old Europe-first "doughface," or Infantryman, as chairman of the Joint Chiefs. A friend asked the Senator in this period, "Did you select the new Chiefs?"

"I wouldn't say *that*," said Taft with a smile. "But I *will* say that before a single new appointment was announced Wilson [Secretary of Defense Charles E. Wilson] had me out to his apartment in the Wardman Park Hotel and showed me the list. I found it entirely satisfactory."

The President himself, still pursuing his policy of accommodation with Taft, told his press conference on May 14 that he had completely turned over the Joint Chiefs as proof of his Administration's new approach and of its severance of the links with the past.

The early spring of 1953, therefore, had brought to Taft great successes as the President's "Prime Minister." He had demonstrated both magnanimity and resolution. He had rebuked the extreme right in the Senate in the Bohlen episode. He had rebuked the "internationalists" (and incidentally the bipartisans) in the Administration in the matter of Yalta. He had seen a changing of the guard at the Pentagon and the departure there of what he thought had been a Europe-first spirit.

He had let the Administration know that it could reckon on nothing without Taft. And he had let the extremists in his own party faction understand that he would not tolerate indiscriminate attacks on the Eisenhower Administration—not even, necessarily, in support of old Taftian notions.

He saw the future open up bright before him. He was coming increasingly to believe that the Eisenhower Administration could work—and still not do violence to the essential orthodox Republican ideas of politics and life. The renunciation of all personal ambition, apart from the agreeably disinterested personal ambition to serve well and largely, had not basically softened his views but it had greatly improved his perspective.

He was acting in a dedicated way. He told Mr. Herbert Hoover in this period that the Eisenhower Administration *must* succeed. If it did not, Taft said, and the country thus did not return the Republicans to the White House in 1956 "we are going as a nation into a long, long slide." The distinct impression gained by many of his friends was that Taft's view of this overriding necessity was impersonal, institutional and ideological and not specially relevant to the

identity of the present White House incumbent, President
Eisenhower.

And as the Senator approached his final task in this spirit
of looking more at a panorama than at the isolated scenes
within it his relationship even with the Senate Democrats
was on the whole an excellent one—and even with the
liberal, or Truman, Democrats. By this time, the most embittered of the Senate's anti-Taftians had begun to accept
Taft for what he was—not his ideas on a dozen great and
small subjects and not his approach to a dozen others but
the fundamental dignity and honor of his life and intentions.

In many ways he showed his essential quality and his
final lack of selfishness; with calm remorselessness he fought
the Democrats but as the Republican leader he would not in
any circumstances permit trespass upon the minority.

Some who had long scorned his cool, lifelong romance
with traditionalism now began to suspect that perhaps there
was something in tradition after all when they saw Taft
indignantly, and not at all for *their* sake, protect their parliamentary rights from the small advantage that smaller men
sometimes sought to take. He would, for example, not permit the majority to bring up a bill unannounced.

This was the spring of Taft's greatest days but before the
season was to run out he was to come, without warning,
upon the last, insoluble crisis of his career, the crisis of
illness and death. And, before the summer could come, he
was to be forced to put down the great burden of power
that so willingly he had assumed.

☆ 21 ☆

THE POLITICAL LAST
TESTAMENT

On June 12, 1953, the dying Robert A. Taft stolidly and carefully made his last will and testament to dispose of a quite unostentatious private fortune that, having been busy with a good many other matters, he had not in many years done much to expand. Characteristically, it was two days before this, that is on June 10, that before arranging his mere personal affairs he made what might be called his political will.

The result of this action, which had no known exact example in the public life of this country, was to leave a vast, complicated political inheritance to a man who was some twenty years Taft's junior, Senator William F. Knowland of California, by a sort of personal handing down of the badges of command.

The differences between the elder and the younger Senator were great, but not so great in fundamentals and certainly not in the greatest fundamental of all: Knowland, in Taft's entirely correct view, was safely Republican and adequately partisan in the traditional way.

These two men were not personally intimate—few were ever really intimate with Taft—but to the one who was about to leave the scene for good this circumstance was simply irrelevant. They had been associated in the Senate, Taft and Knowland, since 1946. And upon the large, earnest, unsmiling form of Knowland Taft had kept a careful eye in his ceaseless search for "safe" young Republicans to whom certain batons perhaps could be passed as time went on.

Knowland's re-election to the Senate in 1952 from one of the largest of the states had been by the largest majority ever given any candidate for any office in California. He had thus not only obtained a most convincing mandate but had demonstrated an extraordinary degree of resultant power within the national Republican organization.

Moreover, and this was to be a highly important point in all that followed, neither in the 1952 Republican Presidential convention nor in all the hard preliminary maneuverings in behalf of this or that candidate had he allowed himself to become really isolated from the Taft people. At the convention he had been at the head of a large and vehement California delegation that was pledged to Governor Earl Warren of that state for the high nomination, and not as a mere favorite son but, as Knowland once remarked, "really meaning it."

The view was general at the time that the Warren people —to whom Knowland was precisely as loyal as Taft had always been to his own local organization—welcomed and sought in all permissible ways to promote and rub up the great Eisenhower-Taft struggle in the notion that *both* might become impossible of nomination and thus that Warren might eventually be chosen.

It was clear that Warren himself (who was, of course, later appointed Chief Justice of the United States by President Eisenhower) was certainly not enthusiastic for Taft and would prefer Eisenhower if the choice became limited to these two. The California delegation therefore was neutral in the Taft-Eisenhower fight only in the most nominal sense of that term; its position, apart from the first fact that it was a Warren delegation, was toward General Eisenhower one of benevolent neutrality.

Knowland himself, however, at this stage was in no sense an Eisenhower man; he contented himself with being just a Warren man. The long and short of it thus was that he was, and correctly so, never identified in the minds of the Taftites with "the Dewey people" who were running the show for General Eisenhower. Knowland, while not ready to support Taft, nevertheless did not wish him any harm. He was wholly protected, by a political tradition that Taft well understood, in confining himself to the Warren movement.

So, when Knowland and Taft returned to Washington in January of 1953 for the new Republican Administration no residual campaign or convention bitterness lay between them. Indeed, Taft's view undoubtedly was that Knowland in staying with Warren to the end had only done what was right in the circumstances.

Knowland allowed himself to be put unofficially in the running for the Senate Republican floor leadership, assuming or preferring to assume that Taft would wish to keep his old post as chairman of the Senate Republican Policy

Committee. This Knowland "availability" only slightly annoyed Taft—who could at all events appreciate its complete candor. He had, it will be recalled, already decided that he himself must take the floor leadership.

While there was never anything in the way of a Taft-Knowland collision, any possibility of that sort was only averted through an accommodation by which Knowland went in as chairman of the Policy Committee (in which Taft had lost a good deal of his old personal interest) and Taft advanced into the floor leadership. The arrangement was in his view an excellent one, if for no other reason than that it made quite certain that no early and all-out Eisenhower man would be able to move in to take the Policy Committee as he moved up to handle matters on the Senate floor.

Knowland, though a coastal Republican, was after all a *West* coast type and thus in Taft's opinion not fatally interlinked with the Eastern, or non-orthodox, group. In a sense, therefore, a "team" was made and though Taft continued to sit in the Policy Committee he was careful never to attempt to run it out of hand and always to leave its functioning to Chairman Knowland. Taft, in the meantime, really kept on making the policy but now he made it elsewhere.

Nothing approaching fundamental disagreement divided the two men. True, Knowland had been far more pro-Europe on foreign policy than had Taft, but he had more than compensated for this failing by his long, dogged preoccupation with the sins and shortcomings, real or alleged, of Democratic policy in Asia. In this field he had been, for most of the time, far out ahead even of Taft; few public men in the United States had done so much so tirelessly to insist on a harder line against the Communists in Asia. And as to domestic affairs, there was no divergence of substance.

In the personal sense, too, Knowland embodied much that Taft had always approved—solidity, a certain stolidity, a gravity of approach that sometimes was very near to humorlessness and, above all, a very deep sense of responsibility accompanied by much of Taft's own brand of political courage.

Therefore, as the spring of 1953 went forward and Taft coolly recognized the accelerating momentum of his fatal illness, he had reached a private decision that Knowland should be his successor. There were others who were much closer to Taft and in the strictly intellectual sense much more like him—for example, Senator Millikin of Colorado—but these were for one reason or another not available. Millikin, for example, is more nearly a political philosopher than a political action man and never had a wish for leadership.

When in May Taft first began to find it necessary to be absent from the Senate for fairly prolonged periods, he turned his front-row seat over to Knowland as the first step in a careful Taft plan for the succession, and Knowland became in fact though not yet by formal designation the acting Republican leader.

Then, on June 10, Taft thought it fit to formalize the position. He sent to the press from his office a statement, nomi-

nally by Jack Martin, his administrative assistant, in which
"Martin" (that is, Taft) declared:

"Senator Taft returned to the Senate today after a further
consultation regarding his hip condition with leading doctors.

"They advised him that the condition is a serious one
and that while he can attend the Senate and keep up his
work there he will have to take a good deal of rest and
pursue a course of treatment which will prevent his being
active as floor leader during the balance of the session."

The fact that the illness had now to be acknowledged as
"serious," an acknowledgment made essential by Taft's purposes in relation to Knowland, was the explanation for the
oblique authority for the statement. It had to be attributed
to Martin because if it had avowedly come from Taft there
could no longer have been any question among his associates
that the end was coming for him very soon. When *he* conceded that anything was "serious" it was most grave, indeed.

Taft went to the Senate floor at noon just as the announce-
ment was being circulated unofficially there and officially
in the press galleries upstairs. He chatted with animation
with one or two old colleagues, in the meantime looking
about him with an air of intent speculation as to what the
general reaction to his admitted semi-retirement would be.

He hobbled on his crutches to his old desk, now occupied
by Knowland, and spoke briefly to the man he proposed
shortly to designate as his successor. He said nothing to
Knowland of future policy, made no suggestion as to how
the Senate's future affairs should be operated, but only said
in an offhand way: "Bill, in a few minutes I intend to have a

press conference and announce that you are to be the acting leader—that is, if it is all right with you."

It was all right with Knowland and shortly Taft met a group of reporters in a lounge off the Senate.

"I have asked Bill Knowland to *go on* as the acting floor leader," he said. "I will continue, however, to be at the Presidential meetings, Policy Committee meetings and so on—unless some specific treatment should prevent that on some specific day."

He then said of Knowland, with a slight, meaningful smile, "*I appointed him.*" It was one of the most illustrative, and at the time least appreciated, examples of the profound parliamentary skill that among other qualities had carried Taft so far in the Senate.

What he had done was to underline that he was not wholly relinquishing the leadership title and he had approached the problem thus because an act of total abdication would have required the *election* of another leader by the Senate Republicans as a group. So long as he insisted that Knowland was only to be "acting" leader this issue could not arise. At the heart of the decision—apart from Taft's calm recognition that his service in the Senate was now drawing fast to a close—was "Mr. Republican's" last desire to avoid at least three eventualities.

First of all, he did not want to see a disorderly struggle within the Republican party for the leadership that he must now put down—and incidentally he was determined to protect Knowland from all avoidable early sniping by the disaffected. Secondly, he was unwilling to accept even the

remote chance that if he retired outright an early Eisenhower man, Senator Leverett Saltonstall of Massachusetts,
might press what would have been a fairly strong claim to
promotion to the leadership, since he long had been serving
as whip, or assistant leader.

And, finally and most important of all, Taft wished to
shunt aside leadership claimants from among the far Republican right wing, even though it was this wing that in all his
career had provided the irreducible base of his followers.

The great change that had come upon him with the first
Republican Presidential victory in twenty years now became plain to those able to understand at all this very
complicated man. As earlier he had all but destroyed the
latent influence in the Senate of the all-out Eisenhower
men, distrusting that influence as one form of extremism, he
now moved in similar distrust to hold static the power of
the right wing.

To turn the Senate hierarchy over to the pro-Eisenhower-
ites would have been emotionally and intellectually impossible for him, because of his institutional view of the Senate
and of the high place of Congress in public affairs. But to
turn the Senate over to the outright anti-Eisenhowerites
(most of whom he certainly preferred, as men) would have
been, for him, equally impossible.

The indispensable point in this thinking, again, went back
to the simple fact that Taft was *determined* that this Republican Administration must succeed. He considered Eisenhower even in the most favoring of circumstances to be
dangerously vulnerable to the designs of far more experi-

enced politicians; to have set the extreme right wing upon the President without restraint would have been to Taft an act of political anarchy not to mention a conspicuous absence of noblesse oblige.

He therefore found, as the end approached for him, the best accommodation that he could find in the circumstances —Knowland. Here was a man who was neither pro-Eisenhowever nor anti-Eisenhower "before Chicago," that is, before the 1952 convention. Here was a man who was genuinely *Republican* and in his way very nearly as singlemindedly so as was Taft himself. Here was a typical "Senate man." Here was a man of strength and stubbornness—not a brilliant man and not, one gathered, accepted by Taft as an intellectual equal, but a man who would not in any circumstance panic in the face of any internal Republican trouble and who certainly would not deal with the Democratic minority any more gently than the circumstances might require.

Moreover, "the Dewey people" were in no sense likely ever to control Knowland.

Taft set about, in sum, in all his pain and in his gallant disregard for the nearing fact of his death, to try to make Knowland the bridge—however shaky and improbable it might sometimes be—that Taft himself had been between the otherwise sundered factions of the Republican party in the Senate.

He took Knowland upon faith and upon observation and without the remotest sense of personal favoritism; while friendly these two were not mutually and deeply sympathetic men in the personal sense. This was the last act of Taft the statesman; the hard, sometimes embittered and narrowly factional orthodox partisanship was now put aside.

The last action succeeded, at least in a limited way, for on the very day of Taft's burial, August 4, 1953, the Senate Republicans officially elected Knowland to the leadership after the collapse of an attempt by right wingers to delay matters and thus to reopen the whole question in January of 1954. Taft's political legacy to Knowland had therefore been validated in its first test, though it was only a beginning and much time must yet run before the shape of the ending will fully emerge.

To President Eisenhower, the real and ultimate legatee, he had left the *hope* at least for an orderly relationship with the Republican party in the Senate; not more than this could he leave.

To his own personal part of the Republican party, the Taft party, he left only the great emptiness of his passing.

☆ 22 ☆

THE ILLNESS AND THE DEATH

I n April of 1953 Taft went to Augusta, Georgia, to golf with
President Eisenhower and shortly after he returned to
Washington his left hip began to trouble him. Always care-
less of his health—he was a heavy, fierce, heedless eater at
dinner, a man who worked appallingly long hours and had
rarely in his life been kept out of action by illness—he paid
no attention for a time to the pain that began to rise sharper
and sharper.

By May, however, the matter could not longer be ignored,
even by Taft, who had now begun to look a little drawn in
the face. He went into Walter Reed Army Hospital in Washington for what was described as a "checkup," and here
began to be issued a long series of cheerful, alternately enigmatic and euphemistic medical bulletins.

Neither the press, the public nor Taft's own closest colleagues paid at first much attention to the course of his
illness; like everything about him it was understated, almost
apologetically, almost until the end. "Taft Progress Satisfactory." "Taft in Good Condition." "Taft Returns to Senate."
"Taft Reported in Fair Condition." These are among the
characteristic headlines of the period, based on the medical

reports. Then there came "Taft in a Coma and Failing Rapidly After Sudden Turn for the Worse."

The date May 23, it now appears, was the day that Taft learned that the outlook was most grave for him. On that day he was released from Walter Reed Hospital after a series of X-ray examinations and treatments that had done nothing to soften the odd pressure of what Taft untiringly called "a lesion of the bone." He went at once home to Cincinnati and to the Holmes Memorial Hospital, from which, it will be recalled, he wrote his last speech.

By this time, toward the end of May, he knew quite well that he was not to go on living much longer and here began the conspiracy of kindness and gentle misrepresentation by which to the end he sought to shelter those who loved him. On June 3, he returned to the Senate floor, supporting himself on crutches, for the first time within two weeks.

He took a seat and beamed whitely at fellow Senators who came by to shake his hand and wish him well. He went home in the afternoon to his house in Washington and, because he thought that a policy of *complete* suppression of fact would be the unkindest policy of all, he said to Mrs. Taft and to Mrs. Darrah Wunder, the old family friend:

"The doctors say it's malignant; but of course they have got all sorts of things to work with now and there is absolutely nothing to worry about." Mrs. Taft, who herself had long been an invalid, accepted this completely, as she had always accepted any Taft statement of fact. Mrs. Wunder was thrown into quiet, and of course unspoken, despair. To even the closest of his political associates Taft meantime was offering a magnificent performance in play acting; he genuinely convinced nearly all of them that his illness was hardly more than a nuisance and the crutches a bit of nonsense with which to humor the doctors.

A few of his friends, however, he did not wholly mislead, and some he did not mislead at all. Because it had been his way always to mellow and seemingly to relax precisely to the extent that his personal affairs were going badly, he had begun, by early June, greatly to worry those who knew this habit of his.

He became extraordinarily gentle and thoughtful—far too gentle and far too considerate for the old Taft. The salt of his occasional ill-temper was wholly missing now; an uncharacteristic sweetness began to be seen in the good acid of this prickly elderly man. And once or twice he took the most alarming line of waving off as of no consequence incidents that normally would have sent him charging onto the Senate floor to correct or to chastise. An undue kindness began to intrude upon his manner.

And while there were those who from all this *suspected* that all was not well there were others who *knew*, and one of these was Herbert Hoover, who had been a kind of mentor to Taft all his adult life. Mr. Hoover, who told me during the preparation of this book that he had always "regarded Bob as a promising young man," was greatly distressed that Taft had not gone earlier, as eventually he did, to physicians in New York.

Mr. Hoover was therefore particularly shocked to find that Taft was to be among the participants in Washington in June of a private conference among certain Republican leaders at which the former President himself was to be on hand.

"I said to him," Mr. Hoover now recalls, " 'Good God, man, you ought not to be here; you ought to stay under treatment in New York!'

"And he said to me: 'I know what I've got and you know what I've got; I'm going to die with my boots on.'

"He was a boy when I first knew him," Mr. Hoover concluded. "And I expect I always looked on him as a boy."

On July 4, all efforts at resisting the disease having failed, Taft re-entered New York Hospital, to which he had first gone in June, now hopelessly and desperately ill—and still denying it to nearly everybody he knew. (He had not denied it to Mack Gray, his colored houseman; he had told Gray: "I only ask the doctors to get me through this Congress.")

By this time Washington and New York alike were alive with rumors that were all too true; that Taft would never return to Washington alive. Now the end inexorably approached; the Senate proceeded in an atmosphere of imperfectly hidden anxiety, much as any family will put about an ailing member. The suggestion was that if one did not talk of the dread thing it might be wished away.

There followed, on July 8, an "exploratory" operation. Taft, who all during this time had been determinedly cheerful and resolutely offhand, remained so to the hour when consciousness left him. Three medical institutions—Walter Reed, Holmes Memorial in Cincinnati and New York Hospital—had now dealt with him and he told his physicians only that they were to do what they thought best and that from him they would hear no carping or complaint.

On the night of July 30 he fell into coma and the hospital bulletin said: "He is failing rapidly." Three of the sons, Robert, Jr., Lloyd and William Howard Taft 3d, were at the hospital. Martha Taft, herself ill and in a wheel chair, had returned to Washington—an instance of the Senator's last touching concern for her.

At 11:30 o'clock on the morning of July 31 his life came peacefully to its close; for thirteen hours he had been in deep coma.

His last months and weeks and days had been a time for shielding others; certainly for two months and probably for longer he had carried within himself the knowledge that he must die. The man who had always demanded "the facts" had known perfectly well since May where he stood with the last fact of all. This fact he faced calmly; he laughed more in the last two months than he had in any ordinary year of his life.

He would permit, as the end approached, no expression of sadness on the faces of his friends; he discussed his illness at all only with great reluctance and when he did it was as though he discussed a minor turn in the weather. This writer last saw him just before his re-entry into New York Hospital in July. He was lying, at this time, on a leather sofa in a small hideaway office he had in the Capitol just off the Senate floor.

"You will be interested to know," he said, "that I have gained back nine pounds."

"Fine. Doesn't that mean you have turned the corner?"

"Yes," he said with an odd smile, "a certain kind of corner, I guess." He was still smiling as I left the room. It was of course clear—later—that in his embarrassed way (always he had great difficulty with any sort of emotion) he had meant to say good-by.

The news of his death struck the Senate just at 11:44 A.M. on July 31 as it struggled wearily and in bad temper with the final business of the first session of the Eighty-third Congress. Senator William F. Knowland of California, Taft's deputy as the Republican Senate leader, was in a routine partisan colloquy with Senator Clinton P. Anderson, Democrat of New Mexico.

A page brought to Senator Lyndon B. Johnson of Texas, the Democratic leader, a slip of paper from the news ticker in the lounge.

"Clint! Clint!" Johnson called softly but urgently to Anderson. "Bob Taft has just died."

Knowland put in a quorum call so that absent members could be summoned. There were tears in Johnson's eyes. Knowland looked almost angry in his attempt to compose himself. All over the Senate men bowed their heads. No greater grief that old chamber had ever known.

President Eisenhower and Mrs. Eisenhower went to the Taft home in Georgetown. There the President took Martha Taft's hand in both of his hands and murmured: "I don't know what I'll do without him; I don't know what I'll do without him."

The tributes that at once came forth were moving; but

perhaps the finest of all came from among men who had opposed Taft the most. Mr. Truman, unable to dissemble just as Taft in reverse circumstances would have been, now declared:

"I am sorry to hear of Senator Taft's death. Senator Taft and I were friends. He and I did not agree on public policy, *but he knew where I stood and I knew where he stood.* His death is a great loss to the country. We need intellectually honest men like Senator Taft. His family has the sympathy of my family and myself."

Mr. Hoover, himself not much of an unbender, issued a public statement that was hardly so eloquent as the tears that long later one saw standing in his eyes when he spoke of Taft:

"Senator Taft was a devoted friend over the thirty-five years since he joined me in public service during the First World War. In all the years he has brought endless blessings to the American people. Senator Taft was more nearly the irreplaceable man in American life than any we have seen in three generations."

President Eisenhower put into the hands of Martha Taft a private letter that is no part of this public story. Publicly, he stated:

"The passing of Robert A. Taft is a tragic loss to America. The brilliant son of our twenty-seventh President, Senator Taft served the people of Ohio and the Nation with distinction and integrity. He will be greatly missed on Capitol Hill, where his vast knowledge of the business of good government played such an important part in Congressional decisions over many years. The Senate has lost one of its leading members of all time. The American people have lost a truly great citizen and I have lost a wise counselor and valued friend.

"Mrs. Eisenhower and I extend to Mrs. Taft and the family our heartfelt sympathies in the personal loss they have sustained."

Mack Gray, the colored houseman, wept. Dr. Johnson McGuire of Cincinnati wrote simply to Mrs. Taft: "Bob's courage in his recent illness surpassed that of any patient I have ever cared for."

The body was taken to the Capitol and there, on the second-floor rotunda, the coffin was put upon the same black-covered catafalque where Abraham Lincoln and William Howard Taft had lain in death. Throughout the day of August 2 and until nine o'clock in the evening, when the lights were put out, thirty thousand men and women and children passed by the catafalque.

On August 3 there was a national memorial service in the rotunda—as old-fashioned as in the days of William Mc-Kinley. There was no radio, no television, and, moreover, no sentimentality of any kind. The light came thin and impersonal through the great dome of the Capitol. The flowers were few and the cool ferns were many.

No one wore formal clothes. The Senators sat together, the members of the House of Representatives sat together. President Eisenhower and Mrs. Eisenhower were there—and so were many others who had been parts of Taft's recent and distant pasts. Many memories stirred. Here one saw General Bradley, who had so lately been deposed by Senator Taft, sitting alongside his successor, Admiral Radford. General MacArthur was there, his thin hands tightly clasped. The British Ambassador, as it happened, sat facing a heroic painting of the British surrender at Yorktown.

The military honor guard about the catafalque was once shifted; a detail of marines was relieved by an all-service detail made up of a soldier, a sailor, an airman and a marine. There was nothing in the way of a strictly religious ceremony —the Episcopal office of the dead was to be read next day in a private burial service on Indian Hill near Cincinnati—but the Senate chaplain, the Reverend Dr. Frederick Brown Harris, thus prayed for the dead Senator:

"Remembering today his towering mind, his transparent sincerity, his unsullied integrity, a grateful Republic now tenderly lifts his familiar form to this exalted pedestal of national honor."

John W. Bricker, the "other Senator" from Ohio, made a small eulogy, stressing rather heavily Taft's religious faith which however deep it may have been he never wore like a cloak. The Marine orchestra played the national anthem, the snare drums rolled and from the Capitol the body was taken by airplane to Cincinnati.

The great circle formed by the rotunda had seen the last unfolding of the tragedy of a man and the tragedy of a time in history. The man's tragedy was that all his exertions and all his sacrifices had never brought him to the place of ultimate leadership that in so many ways he had so honestly earned. The time's tragedy was that this man who in most of his career had been too honest for his era had likewise been too remote from its terrible realities, too uncomprehending of too much to be accepted for that leadership.

The flags of all Washington were at half-staff, and improbable tears were in the eyes of many at this national farewell to Taft. Here had come to a close perhaps the strangest public career in the long life of this country; the story of a unique public official who had, as the term is commonly understood, no political gift at all.

And as the ceremony of burial was said on August 4 on Indian Hill all the United States of America was somehow bereft, whether all of it knew it or not. In a way that is hard to explain a great part of the country was conscious of its sense of loss.

This big, homely, sometimes harsh man with his protruding teeth, this man who never was President and perhaps ought never to have been—it was not only he that was gone. Gone, too, was a good, clean redolence of the past. And every man who valued the brave, the kind, the awkward gallant—never mind, just now, all the great national questions of who was right about this and who was right about that—every such man knew that a special ending had now come.

POSTSCRIPT

AND NOW, THE FUTURE

The death of Robert A. Taft did more than to end one of the most fascinating personal political histories of the United States and to raise great problems before the Eisenhower Administration.

It could almost be said that with him died one kind of Republican party, for he was its head and front, its brain and heart, the personification of its oddly illogical rationale, its reason for being. To speak of the old-fashioned professional Republican party without Taft is like speaking of the old-fashioned Democratic party without the South; he was an embodied force as well as a man. It is almost impossible to see how this party will survive well without him, though even with him it knew mainly the lean days.

Not in seventeen years—that is, not since 1936 and the nomination of Governor Landon of Kansas—had the orthodox Midwest Republicans really wanted other than Taft at their head. They wanted him whether they understood him always or not; sometimes they even wanted him when they did not at all approve of him. He had symbolized their successive defeats at national Republican conventions since 1940. More and more his own failures at convention time had signalized the inability of the home of the Republican party, the Middle

West, to be at home in that party any more. As Taft failed, so progressively declined the influence of the Midwest in the national party.

But, or so it seemed, every one of his own rejections only endeared him the more to these orthodox Republicans; if it came to that, they had rather lose with him than win with another. They saw in him, each to his own eye, all their qualities, all their prejudices, all their hopes. For the strong isolationists, there was quite enough in his record to be appealing. For those in some degree resisting isolationism, something could be found, too, in all his words and actions on the subject. For those whose greatest interest was fiscal stability, there were whole great chapters. For those willing to spend a little bit more here and there in certain circumstances, there were short chapters, too.

And, perhaps most important of all in a human sense, there was about him an aura of profound and unchallengeable respectability. The man whose grandchildren called him "the Gop" (their contraction at once for the Republican party and for the word "Mr. Republican") was far more rigid and formidable in his public face. The very absence of lightness in his public personality was, in this regard, a great help to him; this and the fact that he could always sense the ridiculous but was wholly unconscious of the merely comic.

And the Taft who again and again led the orthodox Republicans to disaster in national conventions nevertheless had been their greatest asset in the last fortress of their power, the Congress. With him, and perhaps even because of him, these Republicans sank steadily in purely *national* power;

but with him they rose steadily in a kind of veto power over the party—their control over the essential functions of Congress through their control of most of the Congressional committees.

It was not only the Taft who put through the Taft-Hartley Act. It was Taft, as the great legislative captain for the orthodox Republicans, who for nearly two decades pressed back and back the hopes and policies not only of the Democrats but of the liberal Republicans, the "modern" Republicans as they called themselves, in their long struggles with him.

He had, when one looks back upon it all, the kind of place that is held by men who are, for the most part, resisting the movement of the present toward the future. For most of the time, his heels were dug in in defense of the past; the fact that his stance was sometimes flexible was significant only in the sense that in a tug of war one sometimes actually improves his position by moving one foot a bit to harder terrain.

The past that nearly always dominates the thinking and actions of the professional orthodox Republicans usually dominated Taft as well. Their unwillingness—and his—to change or to compromise is a part of their nature as it was a part of his.

The hold that he had upon them was never more demonstrated than in 1952 when on the first ballot at the Republican convention in Chicago these professional orthodox Republicans from ten Midwestern states gave him 227 votes to 95 for General Eisenhower. Historically they are known in the political trade—and how aptly!—as "Ohio Republicans," that is, a group basically going back to three Ohio Presidents, William McKinley, Warren G. Harding and William Howard Taft.

And only twice in the last four Presidential elections have Ohio and Illinois, another "Ohio Republican" state, contributed to the Republican column. There is, therefore, a permissible deduction that the Midwestern professionals, those who idolized Taft with a peculiar and genuine personal fervor, perhaps had long since lost touch with the nonprofessional Republican rank and file. It could be argued quite as easily, on the other hand, as Taft liked to argue, that the very fact that the Republican party twice nominated his old antagonist, Governor Dewey, showed on the contrary simply that the controlling Eastern interests had lost touch with Ohio and Illinois.

As for Taft himself, he never had the touch to lose with these controlling Eastern interests, just as he was isolated in the most absolute sense from the wishes and habits of a great body of American voters that he always believed to be "mythical"—the independents. He had an enormous way with him in dealing with other Midwestern Republican professionals; nobody could have been more alien from the independents, whether independent persons or the independent press.

In him, the orthodox resisted to the end what seems to have been a slow, historic turning of the larger, more inchoate, not-altogether-Republican Republican party to views that he could never have followed. That party has come forward to challenge the Democrats with a coalition as unlikely as was the first long-successful Democratic coalition of modern times—that formed by Franklin Roosevelt. Just as Mr. Roosevelt somehow was able to bring together the most right-wing of Southern planters and the most left-wing of Detroit automobile workers, the non-Taft Republicans seem to have formed an odd mosaic made up of a bit of the South, most of the managerial class, millions of people who are "Republican" only in the most limited sense.

With these, Taft never would have found an accommodation, for this sort of coalition was to him so much Sanskrit. The professionally orthodox with whom he consorted could imagine nothing more absurd than a part-time Republican, nor could he. While he would have been hard put to draw up, within reasonable space and without an unreasonable number of qualifications, the proper definition of a Republican, he had what was to him a quite satisfactory instinctual definition.

At the heart of this definition would have been loyalty to party and suspicion of change. Taft, for example, greatly benefited legislatively from the frequent assistance and association of Southern Democrats but even while he appreciated the results of their rebellion he did not think highly of the act itself. His joy in having Mr. Truman as his special foeman was increased, I believe, because he recognized in Mr. Truman a fellow partisan who was prepared to defend his party in every turn and at every risk.

In Taft's last days, while he was yet able to attend the Senate, though on crutches, Mr. Truman returned to Washington for a brief visit and came to the Senate, where he, too, had served. Entering that cheering chamber, he went first and at once to Taft's desk. The Senator arose, though with white-faced difficulty, and grinned. Mr. Truman grinned, too, and caught Taft's hand in a vigorous two-handed clasp. Curious as it may seem, these two had something in common; they fought each and every party fight to its finish. Taft was dying, then, and Mr. Truman was long out of office; they met here as weary warriors, taking nothing back from the past but too tired now for further malice.

Another warrior of the past, General of the Army Douglas MacArthur, may have had something of this past in mind in his letter to Martha Taft after her husband's death. "First and above all else," he said, "Mrs. MacArthur and myself want you to know how real and how sincere and understanding is our sympathy for you in your inestimable personal loss.

"We know that the gaps created by death can never be completely bridged, although a merciful God has ordained that time tends to smooth the way. I think you know of the close political relationship between your husband and myself. I felt he was the indestructible bulwark upon which we could base the welfare and future of our beloved country. Now that he has gone I have an indescribable feeling of national loss that leaves me for the first time in a mood of pessimism for the future. . . ."

This was the feeling of many thousands, perhaps of many millions, not a feeling simply for the loss of a man but for the loss of an era. For Taft in many places—in his part of the Republican party, in the Congressional leadership—had been a movement as well as a person. It is not likely that the orthodox Republicans will soon find his like again and if they find a figure to replace him it can never be an equivalent figure.

For Taft, I think, was this: a highly individualistic man who thought in a highly institutional way. Some who knew him best would have gladly seen him President—if only it weren't for his foreign policy. Some who knew him best would gladly have seen him President—if only it weren't for the associates he picked. He was not, however, totally resistant to changing his mind, granted that the required information reached him, from the right sources. And as President his associations would have broadened vastly.

It is this writer's view that what really closed the door on his last ambition, the White House, was not a lack of generosity and large-mindedness, for both of these he had; but only a lack of understanding. He knew much, but much he did not *understand*. At all events, it is all pointless now; for he never reached the Presidency. All he did was to shape American public life as few men before him had ever done.

The great questions, now that he is gone, are two. What will be the ultimate effect on the Eisenhower Administration and the type of Republican party he represents, and what will be the ultimate shape of Taft's Republican party without Taft?

As to the Administration, its position in the Senate, for the short term at least, will be gravely embarrassed, for with no Taft there will be no center of gravity on the Republican side. It is clear that long and perhaps bitter contentions are likely among those Republicans who will wish to succeed him.

The basic problem, however, is likely to be less obvious but greater. For in the absence of Taft, with all his complicated meaning, what will happen among the fundamental divisions within the Republican party that existed during his lifetime?

There was, in his day, a small faction that was genuinely devoted to the President and ready to follow him in almost any enterprise much as a similar Democratic Congressional group once followed Mr. Roosevelt.

There was a larger faction that was basically anti-Eisenhower, or at best non-Eisenhower, that never willingly recognized President Eisenhower's leadership, except to the extent that this was forced upon them by Taft himself. Finally, there was a third and substantial group, in which Taft most of the time made his own residence (though he moved into and out of the other two groups) that accepted Eisenhower only for the traditional and narrow reason that he had been elected President on a Republican ticket.

To make an amalgam of this inchoate mass had been Taft's great final achievement.

The Administration's immediate problem therefore would appear to be: To raise up before the 1956 Presidential elections the nearest possible and least unacceptable alternative to Taft in the form of a single Republican leader, or to meet the issue head-on and challenge in behalf of the White House all the anti-Eisenhower and non-Eisenhower Republicans.

The enormous difficulty of the first course may be indicated by the simple statement that there was only one Taft and another is not remotely in sight. The dangers of the second course are obvious; vigorously followed it could lead President Eisenhower to a point he has never wanted to reach—open warfare with Congress, or with the Senate at least.

As to the future of Taft's old party the only certainty seems to be that no matter what happens that party will not soon again have anything like the power it had under his unique leadership. There is visible among all the Republicans who had generally his views no other of national stature who has the almost boundless respect of so many men who so disagreed with him in so many ways.

Who else among them, for example, could survive in the Midwest the remarkable candor of Taft's expressed views on the subject of farm subsidies? Who else among them could retain the faithful support of a large part of the American industrial community and so depart from its wishes as he did in the Taft-Hartley Act and elsewhere on occasion?

And aside from this lack of leadership succession for the old Taft Republican party there are obvious dangers that his passing may turn it more and more toward the extremists whom he tolerated and even supported but did not at the end trust as his inheritors. It will be recalled, for example, that Taft had no hesitation in rebuking Senator McCarthy when the question was an attack by McCarthy on the decisions of a *Republican* Secretary of State.

It is therefore possible to suggest that while the problems left to the Eisenhower Administration by Taft's death are complex, the problems left to his old Midwest-based Republican party are insoluble. While the other, or Eisenhower-Dewey Republican party, has existed and can again, on the principle of a varying leadership at the top, the Taft Republican party is disembodied without him.

Though it is entirely possible that reorganized and redirected it may go on, that party as it has existed really lies buried on Indian Hill outside Cincinnati.

Index